IN THE SLENDER MARGIN

IN THE SLENDER MARGIN

The Intimate Strangeness of Death and Dying

EVE JOSEPH

PATRICK CREAN EDITIONS
HarperCollins*Publishers*Ltd

Published by Patrick Crean Editions,
an imprint of HarperCollins Publishers Ltd.

First Edition

HarperCollins books may be purchased for educational, business, or sales
promotional use through our Special Markets Department.

HarperCollins Publishers Ltd
2 Bloor Street East, 20th Floor
Toronto, Ontario, Canada
M4W 1A8

www.harpercollins.ca

Library and Archives Canada Cataloguing in Publication
information is available upon request.

ISBN 978-1-44342-671-8

Printed and bound in the United States of America
RRD 9 8 7 6 5 4 3 2 1

For Ian

On the night we die a thousand others go with us.
—D. J. ENRIGHT, *The Oxford Book of Death*

CONTENTS

ONE   The Basement   1
TWO   Through the Land of the Dying   13
THREE   The Dynamic Corpse   123
FOUR   Death's Confidante   177

          Afterword   201
          Acknowledgements   205
          Sources   207

ONE

The Basement

The Sun will die in its sleep beneath a bridge,
and trailing westward like a winding-sheet—
listen, my dear—how softly Night arrives.

—CHARLES BAUDELAIRE, "Meditation"

A Forbidden Room

I had just turned twelve when my brother was killed in a car accident. In 1965, the year Allen Ginsberg coined the term *flower power* and Malcolm X was shot dead inside Harlem's Audubon Ballroom, the year T. S. Eliot died and Bob Dylan's "Like a Rolling Stone" was on its way to becoming a new anthem, death was regarded as a taboo subject. Not a lot was known about what to do with a kid whose brother had suddenly died on the other side of the country.

It was late evening when the call came. The blinds were drawn against the dark of January and the dog lay sleeping in front of the fireplace. The phone, ringing, at the wrong time, sounded loud, as if ringing in an empty house. My mother's face changed that night. One minute she was reading on the couch, the right side of her face bathed in lamplight, the left in shadow; the next, the phone was in her hand only she wasn't talking into it, she was holding it away from her face and her words were not making sense. I sat sideways on a chair across from her, dangling my legs. My feet didn't quite reach the floor and when she screamed I swung my legs faster as if I were on a swing. That night my mother rocked in a chair and I slept on the floor, curled at her feet. In his diary, Edvard

Munch wrote that he was inspired to paint *The Scream* when he saw the sky turn blood-red while walking along a path with two friends at sunset. "I paused, feeling exhausted, and leaned on the fence—there was blood and tongues of fire above the blue-black fjord and the city—I sensed an infinite scream passing through nature."

I grew up in a house of ghosts. My brother's death followed the deaths of my mother's mother, her father and her brother in the war. When a bomb hit my grandmother's house in London, she was killed by falling debris just as she reached for the gin and tonic my mother was passing to her. Years after the war, a shell fragment pushed its way through my mother's eyebrow; the entry wounds were invisible, but the evidence was compelling. Her stories were like that. It took the rescuers thirty hours to dig through the rubble. Emerging out of the dust like coal miners, they lifted her back into the light of an unrecognizable city. She never learned where they took her mother's body. "None of my deaths," she later told me, "have markers."

My mother's grief over my brother's death reverberated through her nerve endings into the night sky. Inseparable from the infinite, it howled along a stretch of highway thousands of miles away and settled in the bones of her face like Dylan's *ghost of electricity*. It entered her—and me too—like a permanent vibration.

By the 1960s it was generally believed that children needed to be protected and shielded from loss, but this had not always been the case. In the mid-1800s, children were given death kits, complete with miniature coffins and mourning clothes, to familiarize them with death. For girls in particular, dressing their dolls in black and laying them out was a kind of rehearsal for participation in the death rituals of adulthood. Until the twentieth century the preparation of the bodies of the dead occurred mostly in people's homes. In 1909, D. H. Lawrence laid the body of a miner out on the floor in his short story "Odour of Chrysanthemums." Neither the wife nor the mother could forget, as they bathed him, that it was death they worked with: "he was heavy and inert, it was hard work to clothe him." Death was an integrated part of life. People died at home rather than in institutions, infant death rates were high, and life expectancy was much shorter. It wasn't until the 1920s, with breakthroughs in medical care and the rise of the funeral industry, that death and the subject of dying began to retreat into the shadows.

After the Second World War, the influx of women into the labour force and the migration from rural areas to urban centres for work made it increasingly difficult to care for the sick and elderly at home. More and more, the old were sent to nursing homes. With medical advances came the belief that death could be postponed almost indefinitely and was a battle to be fought and won at all costs. What couldn't be fixed was removed from view, and along with what was removed from view, our memories of what to do and how to think about death began to fade as well. In the home I grew up in, death was a well-kept secret; for many years it felt as if I were standing on tiptoes, peeking into a forbidden room.

I spent the time between the phone call and my brother's burial playing with my collection of small plastic horses in the basement. The poet Dorothy Livesay's son, Peter, was attending university and living with us at the time, and it fell to him to stay with me while the adults upstairs struggled over funeral arrangements. I had pintos, mustangs, Appaloosas and coal-black Arabians, and at one point, when the adults were agonizing over burial or cremation, I must have headed out on the dappled paint and made a beeline for the badlands, all of the horses following me, heading to a sheltered valley to set up camp and sleep beneath a million stars that sparkled like five-pointed sheriff's badges.

It was raining the day Ian was buried. Memory is often deceptive; in my mind I was downstairs for days on end, but of course this can't be true. More bewildered than sad, I did not know that grief had taken up permanent residence in our house on the corner of Sixth Street. I did not understand that I was being shaped not so much by grief as by the silence surrounding it. When I eventually surfaced, out of the basement, the funeral was over and everyone had gone home. I watched my mother gather armfuls of lilies and throw them in the trash can.

I see now that our first experiences with loss shape us in ways we don't understand at the time. The death of Sylvia Plath's father when she was eight carved out a small space inside her where the idea of suicide could burrow. In *The Year of Magical Thinking*, Joan Didion writes that, with death, something inside us is dislodged, calved like a piece of sheer blue ice from a glacier. C. S. Lewis suggests that with death there are no lights on in the windows of the house, and we wonder, along with him, if it was ever inhabited.

The archetypal journey to the underworld is one in which the one who is left behind in this world follows the beloved to the land of no return. Orpheus travels to the underworld to attempt to retrieve Eurydice; Hermes goes on behalf of Demeter to bring back her daughter Persephone. There are no maps, no compasses, no sextants with their plates of coloured glass by which to read the stars.

When Ian died, the door to the underworld swung open. I had no idea, when I first studied social work and then went to work for more than twenty years at a well-established hospice, that I was trying to sight the grief of my past experience through the scope of hospice work. To work with the dying is to step out of the known world into the unknown; it was as if death itself had an intimate knowledge of my brother that I could access only by becoming its confidante.

The lilies my mother threw out would have been *Lilium longiflorum*—trumpet-shaped lilies native to the Ryukyu Islands of Japan, the lilies mentioned in the Bible as the white-robed apostles of hope found growing in the Garden of Gethsemane after Christ's crucifixion. Lilies that were said to have sprung up where drops of blood fell.

———————

The Polish poet Adam Zagajewski believes we have at least two kinds of memory: one that synthesizes and encompasses the large themes of our lives and one that he calls her "humbler sister," the memory of little snapshots, quick associations and fleeting glimpses. I was seventeen years younger than my brother; my memories are those of the humbler sister—fleeting, few. Ian worked on the DEW Line in the far northern Arctic for a year when he was nineteen. My mother told me he was briefly a pilot until one time he flew five hundred miles off course and was sent home. By the mid-1950s, jets routinely broke the sound barrier, and whenever a sonic boom hit—rattling our windows and shaking the clothesline—I would point to the sky and say, "E" "E" "E." Sometimes a memory is no bigger than a vowel. A single sound and I see him—a nineteen-year-old god of thunder in his silver cockpit splitting open the skies. The same god who, on a trip south, blew all his wages on a Rolex watch and got briefly engaged to Miss Canada.

Twenty-eight when he died, thin and dark-haired with high cheekbones, he had a kind of rangy beauty—part Kerouac, part altar boy. He was beautiful, unfit, often drunk and blazingly intelligent. After completing his master's thesis in English in 1962, he left for Toronto to study with Northrop Frye. He shone like the silver I took out of its red velvet case and polished every Sunday. As we have all aged, he has remained pinned in our imaginations as a young man with all the vitality and recklessness of youth—more alive in death than he ever could have been in life.

When I was a young girl, I fell in love with poetry one afternoon in grade five. My teacher, Mrs. Black, leaned back against her desk and read to us from Shelley, Keats, Byron and Blake. Time slowed, the way it slows when people describe an accident or trauma, and I remember thinking I could actually taste the words she was saying. After what was an archetypal thunderbolt experience, I wrote into my early twenties and then stopped for thirty years. When I returned to poetry, having worked with the dying for many years, I realized how the two things were twinned. I met my husband, Patrick, at the late poet Al Purdy's eightieth birthday party. We stood in a doorway talking about death and poetry long after the last guest had left. The borders between the two are blurred: the language of both is metaphor. Mythology, legend, imagination and poetry grow out of the same black soil as death. All exist beyond the frontiers of logic. It was to these things that I turned to try to find my way out of the basement.

THIRTY YEARS AFTER MY BROTHER DIED, I CAME ACROSS A POEM *by George Bowering, a friend of his, in which I learned that his body had been shipped across Canada by train in a blue casket. The train idled on the prairie four miles from where Bowering lay sleeping before it disappeared into the Rockies on its way to the West Coast.*

Why this story stays with me I can't fully explain. Until I read the poem, I had not known that Ian's body was shipped across the country by rail. The last image I have of him in my imagination is of him lying on a road outside Toronto. It is quiet, and the smell of clover from a nearby ditch fills the night air. Of course, when I think about this, I know it is impossible. He died in January, in the heart of winter; there would have been snow and ice. Summer with its sweet smells was months away.

There was no meaning to be had in Ian's death. It was not his time; it was not meant to be or a sign of God's plan. It was an accident. A mishap. My mother's hope was as thin as a Giacometti sculpture: from hoping he'd take his muddy shoes off in the hallway and sit down at the supper table, to hoping he'd go to school, get married, have babies—from her hopes and her dreams for him—in the end she hoped he had died quickly. When a friend called the coroner in Toronto and found out that he had been killed instantly, my mother was grateful. It is not possible to take in such a hope. Are we deepened by sorrow or depleted by it? We hope to be spared the knowledge; we never imagine that we will hope for the unthinkable.

There is a story about a tribe of nomads crossing the Sahara Desert who pause every few hours in order to let their spirits catch up with them. It seems right that it took my brother five days to arrive at the place he would be buried, right that he came across the country in a casket the colour of the sky.

TWO

Through the Land of the Dying

These be
Three silent things:
The falling snow . . . the hour
Before the dawn . . . the mouth of one
Just dead.

—ADELAIDE CRAPSEY, "Triad"

We Played at Death As If It Were a Game

When I was six, I roller skated home so fast sparks flew from the backs of my skates. In my hand was the still-warm, limp body of a yellow budgie that I had retrieved from the floor of its cage at my best friend Kathy's house. The bird felt weightless and soft as talcum powder. I didn't know what death meant, but I knew it was big.

The street I grew up on in North Vancouver was a small world bordered by the Gilmores on one end of the block and the Rankins on the other. On summer nights it was Susan, Kathy, Glenda and I against Alan, Gary, Kenny and Ryan; we stocked our arsenals with hard red mountain ash berries and fired at each other with homemade slingshots. We pranced around with silver wands and strapped on fairy wings made of tin foil and cardboard and dressed up as cowboys and Indians and shot each other dead with silver pistols carried in holsters slung low over our hips. And then we went home for dinner. In our world, the dead didn't stay dead for very long.

One minute the budgie was singing, the next it was lying in the sawdust. Neither my friend nor I saw it fall. It's a kind of magic trick that birds do.

In the early 1950s, Mao Zedong declared war on sparrows. The Chinese were exhorted to bang drums, pots, pans and gongs in order to keep the birds flying until they fell, exhausted, to the earth. Shanghai alone accounted for over one million dead sparrows. The death of over five thousand birds on New Year's Eve 2010 in Beebe, Arkansas, was likely caused by fireworks that sent thousands of panicked red-winged blackbirds into such a tizzy that they crashed into homes, cars and each other before plummeting to their deaths. Over the years I have seen many dead birds—crows on the lawn, gulls at the side of the road, headless robins dragged into the house by the cat—but I have never seen a bird die. Never seen one fall out of the sky.

Along with the yellow budgie, I buried birds that flew into our windowpanes and goldfish that floated belly up in their glass bowls, in my backyard. I dug holes with my mother's silver spoons and made little crosses out of Popsicle sticks. I also carried a bouquet of wildflowers and practised walking slowly like a bride. Unlike the Italian women, who dressed in black from head to toe and walked slowly along the sidewalk hunched over like crows in front of our house, I had no visible way to show my grief. My first funerals for animals were shaped not by belief in a send-off to the afterlife but out of love of ceremony: the little graves, the procession and the tea party on the lawn afterwards. My earliest funerals were like weddings.

My friends and I played at death as if it were a game like frozen tag or Mother-May-I. Six months after my brother died, Kathy's father and uncle were swept away in the Nechako River where they had been fishing. Every day I waited to hear if their bodies had surfaced. I imagined myself washed away and devised ways to save myself from the churning waters of my own imagination. I practised holding my breath underwater and visualized grabbing an overhanging branch and hauling myself out of the rapids. I lay perfectly still on my bed with my hands crossed on my chest. Summer passed without any news; I started grade five and stopped playing dead. In the past, when he was home, Kathy's dad would drop on all fours and pretend to be a big black bear. He lumbered through the halls with us squealing ahead of him. I can't remember what he looked like as a man, but I clearly remember him as a bear. I never saw Kathy cry; she waited without ever talking about what she was waiting for. Once inseparable, by fall we started to drift apart.

My brother eloped when he was twenty-five and moved to Toronto with his bride, Dee. Before they left, he took me to meet her parents at their cranberry bog in Richmond. I don't recall much about the day other than the floating fields of red and my brother wading waist-deep through them.

A couple of months after Ian died, Dee arranged for me to come to Toronto. Every morning I walked to the red postbox at the end of Isabella Street to mail a letter home to my mother. Afternoons we visited their friends, Beth and Wally. Wally plunked me on the counter and made special fruit drinks in a martini shaker and served them to me with a maraschino cherry and a paper umbrella on top. Dee had started packing up the apartment before I arrived; cardboard boxes were stacked up against the bare walls and we both slept on a mattress on the floor. She took me to the Woodbine Racetrack and stood with me at the betting window, where I placed two dollars on a black stallion to show and we watched my horse come last, through little opera glasses. I have no idea why she sent for me. I've wondered if she saw a little of Ian in his kid sister. I've wondered if she felt she could hold on to him a little longer if I was close by. Grief is inarticulate. We didn't talk about him the whole week I was there.

"Why isn't the earth littered with the bodies of birds?" my daughter asked me when she was eight. Why indeed. When I started working at hospice, I had never seen a dead body; I had never seen anyone die. Like the birds I had never seen fall out of the sky, the dying were invisible.

Friendliness to Ghosts

In Greek mythology, Hades is the Lord of Death, Thanatos is Death itself—son of Nyx, goddess of night, and Erebos, god of darkness—daimon of non-violent death who lives with his twin brother, Hypnos, the god of sleep, in a cave surrounded by opium poppies. The hour is always twilight, the only noise the slow trickling of the river Lethe, the river of forgetfulness. Thanatos is sometimes portrayed as a winged bearded man, other times as a beautiful winged boy. His touch is gentle, likened to that of his brother who lies on his soft couch, surrounded by his many sons, who are the bringers of dreams.

Sometimes we can't tell the twins apart: comforting ourselves by saying the dead look as though they are sleeping. Praying, as we fall asleep, that we don't die before we wake. "Death was a friend," wrote Steinbeck, "and sleep was death's brother."

In the Judeo-Christian tradition, the Grim Reaper is a dark, hooded, skeletal figure who carries a large scythe that he uses like a well-honed razor blade to collect souls. In Europe during the Middle Ages, children were dressed as adults as soon as possible to trick death into looking elsewhere for prey. The Angel of Death, according to Jewish lore, has twelve wings and is said to be "full of eyes." There is no hiding from him. From the beginning of recorded history, we have painted, danced, sung and written about death. We have dressed as devils, skeletons, reapers and ghosts on the night of All Hallows Eve and eased our fears by holding out our pillowcases for strangers to fill with sweets in the night.

In the Downtown Eastside of Vancouver, home to the city's most vulnerable citizens, Thanatos has been working the streets since 2008. He dresses as a superhero, his dark costume a mix of the Green Hornet, The Shadow, Doc Savage and Batman. Along with a black and green mask, he wears a long trench coat, a skull-and-crossbones tie and a wide-rimmed black hat. A former military man, Thanatos moved to Canada from the States in 1973, naming his alter ego after the Greek god of death. In a cemetery in Vancouver, Thanatos talked to a reporter from the *Globe and Mail* about how he tries to help the homeless. Along with the water, food and blankets he hands out, he also gives white strips of paper with the word *friend* written on them. "It's better to have a friend in a costume," he says, "than to have no friend at all." From a cave on the river Lethe to Hastings and Main. From the river of forgetfulness to the forgotten. Try as I might, I could not make this up.

———————

The word *hospice* was first used in the fourth century by monks who welcomed and provided sanctuary for pilgrims. During the Crusades, these guesthouses took in weary travellers and served as places of refuge for orphans, lepers and the destitute. It wasn't until the mid-1800s in France, when Jeanne Garnier founded the Dames du Calvaire hospice in Lyon, that the name became exclusively associated with the care of the dying, shortly after which Our Lady's Hospice was opened by the Sisters of Charity in Dublin.

Derived from the Latin *hospitium*, meaning both "host" and "guest," hospice is an idea as well as a place. In Homeric times all strangers were regarded as guests; the obligation to be hospitable to strangers was imposed on civilized man by Zeus himself—one of whose many titles was Xenios, "protector of strangers." In the *Odyssey*, Alcinous, king of the Phaeacians, offers hospitality to Odysseus without knowing who he is: "Tell him, then, to rise and take a seat on a stool inlaid with silver and let the housekeeper give him some supper, of whatever there might be in the house."

When I look up the root for *hospitality*, I misread "friendliness to guests" as "friendliness to ghosts" and think this is not entirely inaccurate. It has been said, by those who can see, that the dead walk the corridors of hospice: mothers holding hands with daughters, brothers, grandfathers and grandmothers, husbands waiting for wives, and others nobody knows, who are just there waiting.

One year before AZT became available and the death rate from AIDS dropped dramatically, a young man dying of AIDS pointed to a couch in his bedroom and warned me not to sit on it.

"Be careful," he said, "not to sit on the old woman."

"What is she doing here?" I asked.

"Knitting," he replied. Too weak to raise his head, he motioned me over with his hand.

"Do you think that means death is near?" he asked.

I glanced at the empty couch. "She brought her knitting," I said. "I think you have a bit more time."

When I met his father, eight months after the death, he told me the only time he felt at peace was when he was flying in a plane. At cruising altitude he was 37,500 feet closer to heaven and his boy than when he was on earth.

The modern hospice as we know it did not come into being until 1967, when St. Christopher's Hospice was opened in south London by Cicely Saunders, a young physician previously trained as a nurse and social worker. The phrase *dying with dignity* became a rallying cry for those working with the dying. The term *palliative*, from the Latin *palliatus*, meaning "to cover with a cloak," was first introduced in 1975 by oncologist Dr. Balfour Mount when he opened a ward for the dying in Montreal. Contemporary medical care of the dying has its roots in the impulse to take the shirts off our backs and cover the sick or injured lying by the side of the road.

Palliative care contains both comfort and concealment. It does what it can to alleviate symptoms and provide a quality of life; at the same time, dying is separated and cloaked in secrecy. Most people, I found, didn't know anything about hospice until they needed it. There is a wonderful audacity to the idea of palliative care—a utilitarianism inherent in a practical response to suffering. Roll up your sleeves and get on with it: one by one, help the dying. *About suffering they were never wrong*, wrote Auden,

> *The Old Masters: how well they understood*
> *Its human position; how it takes place*
> *While someone else is eating or opening a*
> *   window or just walking dully along.*

If my brother's death led me to my life in the death business, pragmatism got me hired. It was 1985 and I was a new social worker with a baby, a six-year-old and a husband who made his living carving large totem poles in our driveway out of yellow cedar logs he salvaged from the beach. In the year that the U.S. Food and Drug Administration approved the first blood test for AIDS and British scientists discovered a hole in the earth's ozone layer, we lived on a dead-end street in Victoria with a massive moss-covered rock at the end of the block that the neighbourhood kids called "the mountain." The largest hospice on the island was a ten-minute walk away, and we were broke. It had never occurred to me to work with the dying; when I walked the few blocks to hand in my application, I wasn't thinking how cathartic or traumatic it might be to work with death, I was thinking, This is great, I can come home for lunch!

It is a complicated thing to be employed to help people

die. On the one hand, each situation, each person, is unique and each death a profound experience; on the other, it is a job, a way of paying the mortgage and supporting a family. You set your alarm to wake up and grab a coffee on the way to work. Traffic is bad and you know the last parking spot is going to be gone. You vow again to leave earlier, but that never happens. Tolstoy wrote, in *War and Peace*, that if a relative was sick, the custom was to seek professional care; but when a close loved one was dying, the custom was to send the professionals away and care for the dying within the family. There was always a grandmother, an aunt or a cousin dying in a room upstairs. Like living in a cave with a sleeping dragon, we once knew how to coexist with what we feared most, unlike today, when we fear not only the fiery breath of death but any mention of it. People who work with the dying are doing work that was traditionally done by families. These days, the dying are most often cared for by strangers—intimate strangers.

The Bay Pavilion, where I first began working, was a one-storey horseshoe-shaped building constructed around a garden. On sunny days some patients sat outside on the deck, and occasionally someone would ask to sleep outside. There were roses, geraniums, nasturtiums, delphiniums and daisies in the rock beds beneath the windows. In the spring, cherry trees transformed the place into a Japanese courtyard; in the fall, the maples turned fire-engine red. These days they call hospice gardens "healing gardens." Back in 1985, the garden made no such claims; a gardener's garden, its *raison d'être* was to revel in its own beauty. For some patients, it was the garden of their childhood; for others, it was the garden they'd always wished they had.

In one of the rooms facing the courtyard, cherry blossoms blew in through an open window and fell on a woman, in her early thirties, who was sleeping. I was in the room with her husband, whom I had met only moments before, when he collapsed in my arms and said, "If there is a God and this is His plan, how can I ever believe in that God again? And if there is no God, how can I live?" I was new to the work and had no answer for him. I hadn't even begun to formulate the questions. I remember looking at her pale skin and black hair and thinking she looked like Snow White in a Red Cross bed. Her window, like all the others on the unit, was kept slightly open to let the spirit leave.

To "begin," from the Old English *bi* and *ginnan*, means "to open, open up." My early days and weeks were spent acclimatizing to the idea of being around the dying. I was struck by the ordinariness of it all: nurses came and went casually from patients' rooms, doctors joked easily with each other, undertakers—their minivans idling at the back door—appeared like specialized delivery men when called. The smells and sounds of death were a kind of muzak—not loud but always in the background. A faint sweetness hung in the air: a tinge of marigold and fetid water. The few people who were still able to rise from their beds were sinew thin, and the ones in their rooms were often short days away from death. I hadn't been there very long when I noticed a smell of rot coming from one of the rooms. Over the next few days I learned that the patient in that particular room was a young woman with a fungating breast tumour that was eating its way through her flesh. I recoiled inside when I heard this and felt grateful I didn't have to go into that room. I did not yet know how diabolical and inventive cancer could be. I knew, as we all do, that people died; I had just never given much thought to how they did it.

Cherry trees blossom in February in Victoria in a kind of mockery of winter. There were times, on my way home from a shift, when it seemed to me as if the seasons were accelerating for those who would not see the coming spring.

God is not omnipotent, says Rabbi Harold Kushner. In times of great difficulty, He weeps with us. That might be so, but for the man who fell into my arms as his wife lay dying in the Bay Pavilion and I stood in the room, trying to make myself small, as he begged her not to go, God's tears were not going to cut it. We need consolation, says the good rabbi, not answers. "Why?" cried the man. "Why?" To which we all waited silently for a few minutes, as if there might be an answer forthcoming from somewhere. An explanation, at least.

I spent hours, in those first weeks and months, with the woman who hired me. In her early sixties, Jo had thick white hair and an open, frank face that creased easily with amusement. She wore cotton dresses and sandals and valued instinct over protocol. In the mid-1980s, hospice was still relatively new; there was a sense of excitement and possibility, and we all felt it. Jo's shelves were filled with books by Carl Jung, Elisabeth Kübler-Ross, Joseph Campbell, Stephen

Levine, Ram Dass, J. William Worden, Therese A. Rando and other volumes on psychological archetypes and mythology. She lent me *Words as Eggs* by Russell A. Lockhart with a seriousness that indicated the book held a key to unlocking the secrets of the dying. I couldn't make heads or tails out of it. There were no set protocols yet; signs proclaiming that foul language or violence would not be tolerated were not yet posted on the walls of health care facilities, including hospice. There was still time to sit with patients who were frightened or restless, and although there was a waiting list to get into hospice, once patients were admitted, there was no pressure to move them to another facility if their dying was prolonged.

One of the first patients I met was a twenty-eight-year-old woman with a rare form of bone cancer. In the weeks preceding her death, the bones of her rib cage were so brittle that one or two broke whenever she rolled over. I was horrified to learn that our bones could snap like twigs.

At birth, a newborn baby has approximately three hundred bones, while on average an adult has two hundred and six. Our bones fuse as we grow; we are building our scaffolding without even knowing it. The twenty-four long, curved bones of our rib cage form a structure that shelters the heart, lungs, liver and spleen. Like exotic birds, we live within the safety of our bony cages.

I talked to Jo about how distressed I felt, and as we walked beneath a canopy of chestnut trees in front of the hospice unit, she talked to me about what it might be like to be trapped inside a body that was breaking apart. "Each bone breaking," she said, "is a possible opening." In the days preceding death, I watched as Jo and the young woman talked about how the cage cracking was the only way she could fly free. Each bone that snapped made the doorway a little wider. For her immediate pain, the young woman was on a morphine drip with breakthrough doses given subcutaneously through a butterfly in her upper arm. She used morphine to get on top of the pain and metaphor to try to understand it.

There is such a fine line between imposing meaning and allowing it to surface naturally. Jo had a fearless mind. I saw, in those hours I spent watching and listening, how she used language as a key to unlock the dying process. I was meeting the dying, but it was death itself I was being introduced to. A figure, a presence, a seduction and a terror. Sometimes merciful, sometimes brutal. I was slowly learning a new language. Slowly learning to see in new ways. What Jo offered as possibility, the young dying woman embraced as her own. I was unsure, even if I had a key, what door it might open and what I would possibly do if it did.

Traditionally, healers often lived on the outskirts of the village. Shamans, prophets, tricksters, magicians, holy men, eccentrics, crazy men and women all had specific roles to play as mediators between the living and the dead. There were times, over the years, when I thought that's what we needed: huts on the edge of the city where people would approach with stories, scraps of memory, a goat, a sack of potatoes, a basket of eggs, a chicken. Places where people like Jo would be revered and feared and the dead could go about their business undisturbed.

The Bay Pavilion was torn down not long after I began working there. The hospice that replaced it is located on the third and fourth floors of an old maternity hospital not far from downtown Victoria. In 1979, the year United Nations Secretary Kurt Waldheim proclaimed as the Year of the Child, I gave birth to my first child in one of the rooms I would help people die in six years later. My memories of life in that room are stronger than those of death. I remember the sensation of falling in love with my new daughter: the quick jerk of it, the way one sometimes catches oneself from falling backwards into sleep to keep from disappearing into the void.

We die alone more than we used to. We rely more on strangers. Good people, with good intentions, who escort us out. We often die in beds that are not our own in rooms with no family photos on the walls; no parlour in which to pay our respects. Far from the caves, huts, hovels and rooms in family homes that we once arrived in and departed from, birth and death have become estranged from each other.

There are seventeen beds on the new unit, seven of them designated for patients with complex symptoms not adequately controlled at home, nine allocated for patients with "weeks to short months" to live, and one for respite care that can be used by patients in the community for up to one week. The average stay, from the time of admission to death, is less than three weeks. When you step out of the elevator on the third floor, you pass a small table with fresh flowers to the left and a large hand-embroidered memorial quilt on the wall above it. On the right is a small glass window containing objects from the Hospice Thrift Shop—jewellery, scarves, pretty vases and dishes, clothes and purses. A friend who works on the hospice unit says that people like to go "shopping" there. She has seen patients buy a necklace for a daughter or granddaughter and others who pick up small mementoes for the person who is dying. It is, my friend says, a small window of normal.

More than three hundred volunteers with various skills work at hospice. Some sing, some play piano in the family lounge, some know reiki and therapeutic touch; many of them make tea and sit with the dying in their rooms. For patients who wish to leave behind some kind of record of their lives, there are volunteers trained to record those stories and memories onto audio CDs. They come from all walks of life: they are doctors, teachers, filmmakers, waitresses, beauticians, dog trainers, painters and potters, CEOs, cops and widows. Some are still working, some retired. There aren't a lot of young volunteers; this is not their country yet.

A man dying of leukemia once asked me if I did anything useful. In his last months he had built a farmer's market on his land so that his wife and four sons would be able to support themselves after his death. Without thinking, I answered that I baked loaves. It was a lie, but it became a fortuitous lie. He told me to bring my loaves to the market and said his family would keep half the money; the other half was mine. The first month after his death, I decided I'd do what I'd told him and made five hundred dollars selling banana, chocolate, blueberry, pumpkin, apple and zucchini loaves. I followed recipes, I made them up. I baked loaves at midnight, wrapped them in tin foil with masking tape labels, and delivered them to the market before going to work in the morning. A few years later, when my marriage ended,

I supported myself and my children with money from the loaves I sold at the man's market.

Sometimes, when I visited patients at home, I'd see one of my loaves wrapped in silver on the kitchen counter. Counselling isn't tangible; it's often difficult to know what, if anything, helps. A slice of chocolate bread with butter melted on it, on the other hand, was, on occasion, the best thing going.

To be with the dying is to wade into mystery. On my first visit as a counsellor with the palliative response team—a team comprising a nurse and a counsellor who provide crisis intervention in patients' homes—an emaciated, naked woman stood on the dresser beside her bed and flung a bottle of perfume at my head; she thought she was in the war and her arsenal consisted of little coloured bottles of eau de toilette. She had captured the ridge and was there for the long haul. Two injections of Haldol by the nurse eventually cleared the woman's delusions, but what helped me to understand what the woman was seeing on that ridge and to talk her down into the safety of her bed—the "bunker" we called it—were my mother's stories of the war and its visceral presence in our lives. Whenever a thunderstorm rolled in over the North Shore Mountains, my mother dove under her bed and plugged her ears until the storm passed and I knelt down to give her the all-clear.

Mona

The origins of *mentor* are lofty. The goddess Athena, disguised as Odysseus's trusted friend Mentor, guided Telemachus in search of his father in the *Odyssey*. The name is proverbial for a faithful and wise adviser. My mentor just happened to have the insignia of a winged death's head skull on the back of her jacket.

Shortly after I started working at hospice, I received a call from a cousin whose six-year-old son was dying of leukemia, asking me to help the family. I was thirty-two years old and new to the work, and I was afraid people would look to me as the expert when, in reality, I felt anxious and unprepared. When I arrived at the house, I was surprised by the laughter I heard coming from the living room and by people milling about without any apparent distress. Eli was lying on a couch beneath a brightly coloured blanket he and his mom had picked up in Tijuana on their last visit to a laetrile clinic in Mexico. His collection of stuffed monkeys made of old grey and white socks with brightly stitched red mouths and button eyes lay draped in various positions around him. By the time I arrived, he was in a coma and breathing irregularly. With his steroids discontinued, his face, which had become round like a full moon, was slowly returning to its natural shape; the closer he got to death, the more he looked like himself. Unsure what to do, I busied myself clearing dishes and making coffee. His breaths were wet and my chest tightened with each one he took.

Around midnight a motorcycle pulled up in front of the house and Eli's auntie pushed open the front door and shook herself off like a wet dog in the hallway. Mona was a junkie and a biker. The last time I'd seen her, she'd stolen forty dollars out of my wallet while I was sleeping. She grew up on reserve in the Squamish Valley in the shadow of the Chief, the second-largest rock in the world. Legend has it that when a piece of granite breaks off and rolls like thunder down the left side of this rock, a death will follow. Mona wore leather pants and a buckskin jacket and had the word *love* tattooed in blue ink across the knuckles of her right hand and *hate* tattooed across the left. In the past she'd pierced her ears the old way, by numbing them with ice cubes and passing a sewing needle, heated over a lighter, through her earlobes and then pulling thread through to keep the holes open.

I watched as she walked down the hallway and up the three carpeted steps to where Eli was lying. She removed the pillow beneath his head, repositioned a couple of monkeys and settled herself down with his head on her lap. She cleaned inside his mouth with a peppermint mouth swab and cooed to him and rocked him and cradled him and loved him and did everything I was afraid to do. She made herself at home in death's house and put her feet up on death's coffee table. "You go, baby," she said. "Whenever you're ready, you just go. They're here. Everyone, they're all waiting for you."

Shortly before he died, there was a loud crack as if a piece of granite had broken off a gigantic rock. Moments before, I had gone to sit in the kitchen as I didn't want my anxiety to hold him back. Eli's First Nations uncle, Len, gathered people in a circle around his body to sing a farewell song; his Christian grandmother sang "Amazing Grace." When he finished singing, Len put down his drum and told us that the crack we had heard meant that the heavens had opened and Eli was in the arms of the Creator. An hour later, when the funeral home came, Mona lifted his body off the couch and gently placed him, wrapped in his blanket, on the gurney.

I would spend my years at hospice trying to be as brave as the thief and biker who arrived like a drenched angel, on the back of a Harley, in the middle of a stormy night.

MY BROTHER LEFT HOME WHEN I WAS JUST A KID. I REMEMBER HIS *black hair and chiselled cheekbones and the way he bounded up the stairs three at a time. When he was studying English literature at UBC, he took me to the old house he rented on Point Grey Road near the university. His room, on the top floor, was cramped with books piled on every surface and seemed to me to be a kind of castle turret. He threw a red blanket over my head and tackled me and we laughed and went down to the beach together, where he made a fire and we roasted marshmallows on sticks. Later that day, he showed me some empty cages that had been built around the outside of the house at ground level. The cages, eight feet tall by six feet wide, were littered with old peanut shells and were used, he told me, for gorillas the circus no longer had any use for. I don't know what the cages were really used for. It never occurred to me to question him; even now, I can imagine my brother falling asleep to the grunts and barks of the great apes filling the city streets with the cries of the jungle.*

Names

Every year, between eight and nine hundred people die on the Victoria Hospice program. In 1985, we gathered once a week in the garden to ring a bell and read out the names of those who had died that week. A friend, who started working as a counsellor shortly before I left, says the names are no longer recited and she can't remember when the practice stopped.

What do we do when the names keep piling up? Each year, 60 million people die. The year my mother died, we decided to have Christmas away from home. On Sunday, December 26, 2004, we were skiing down Mount Washington through drifts of new snow when the Boxing Day tsunami killed 230,000 people in Southeast Asia.

In Washington, D.C., 58,267 names are written on black polished granite on the Vietnam Veterans Memorial—"the Wall" as it is otherwise known. At Sunset Beach, a short walk from Stanley Park on English Bay, the names of those who have died of AIDS in the city are cut through twenty steel panels on a wooded slope. The same wooded slope where I wove daisy chains to wear on my wrists and ankles in the mid-sixties. In the spring, when you stand with your back to the ocean reading the names, you can look through each one to the purple crocuses growing on the bank. In the winter, when it snows, each letter is a perfect white stencil. When you go to the website for the Vancouver AIDS Memorial Society, you will see that a lack of funding and volunteers leaves them unable to operate any longer.

"What," asks Annie Dillard, "what will move us to pity?"

My husband, Patrick, grew up on the prairies. His grandmother, Maria, who lived in a small Mennonite community just north of Steinbach, Manitoba, was one of 50 million people who died of Spanish flu in 1918. When she was ill, people brought food and left it on her doorstep, not wanting to catch the disease themselves. The day Maria died, the family carried her body past her house; her mother raised herself on one elbow to see her daughter pass by on the way to the grave before she, too, died the next day. The word *influenza*, first used in Italian, has its origins in the belief that epidemics were due to the influence of the stars. An ethereal fluid, flowing from the heavens, was believed to directly affect the "character and destiny" of men.

In the late 1800s, smallpox bloomed up the west coast, killing half the Native population from Victoria to Alaska. At Fort Victoria, a Hudson's Bay trading post to which Native hunters and trappers came from all over the province, whites were immunized against smallpox; Natives weren't. When we fall sick, we head for home. One of the legends of the Kwantlen people tells of a fearful dragon with eyes of fire and breath of steam who lived not far from the village. When this dragon awoke and breathed upon the children, sores broke out where his breath had touched them and they burned with heat and they died to feed this monster. During the smallpox epidemic, the Kwantlen people along the Fraser River paddled softly so as not to wake the sleeping dragon. Is it any surprise we stop writing down the names and ringing bells?

———————

An infinite number of things die every minute, writes Borges: "Events, far-reaching enough to people all space, whose end is nonetheless tolled when one man dies, may cause us wonder." We feel for one what we cannot feel for many. Every so often my mother would stop in the middle of whatever it was she was doing and imagine what Ian might have looked like as a middle-aged man; other times she'd say, "I would have grandchildren by now," and she'd calculate their ages. She used to tell the story of how she sailed from London to New York to join her husband, John, on the maiden voyage of the *Queen Elizabeth* with two young children in tow, and how, on the train across Canada, the prairie was covered in a sea of yellow rapeseed. They arrived in Vancouver on October 31, 1946. My sister was two, but Ian was old enough to go out trick-or-treating. He wore his British schoolboy's outfit; people thought it was the greatest costume they'd ever seen.

Rough estimates indicate that over 108 billion people have died in human history. The living will never outnumber the dead. The World Population Clock, which operates continuously, currently estimates that each second 4.3 people are born and 1.8 people die. Of the 52 million people who die every year, 150 are killed by falling coconuts, which, if true, makes the tropical fruit about ten times more dangerous than sharks.

I remember the names of the patients I met early more readily than I do the later ones. When the names became too many, I remembered faces; when the faces overwhelmed, I remembered people by the diseases they died of: the man on the farm who died of Lou Gehrig's, the baby with the glioblastoma, the sailor with throat cancer, the cyclist with bone cancer. The actress in a green velvet dressing gown with a tumour growing in the shadow of her heart.

This morning I wake up wondering what the name *Ian* means. In an online reference I find it is the Gaelic form of *John*. I didn't know he was named after his father. In Scottish, the name means—"Gift from God."

Only now does it occur to me that he made two train trips across the country: one when he arrived, as a boy, through fields of yellow; the other in a box the colour of the prairie sky.

The world's seven-billionth person, Danica May Camacho, was born in the Philippines on October 31, 2011—sixty-five years to the day after my mother arrived with her two children from England and my brother headed straight out into the goblin- and ghost-filled streets of his new home.

Taming Death

I recently read a description of a local creek that has changed the way I hear water. *Colquitz Creek*, named by the First Peoples of the area, translates roughly into "baby crying and crying until it is exhausted and no one is going to comfort it." There is an inconsolable quality to water that I didn't recognize until I heard it named.

Prior to the 1969 publication of *On Death and Dying* by

thanatologist Elisabeth Kübler-Ross, a great silence prevailed in North America. Death was denied description because it was denied expression. As a society, we bury our dead and yet often refuse to let them die. There have been thousands of sightings of Elvis since his death. At the funeral, his father, Vernon, allegedly acknowledged that the corpse in the coffin did not look like his son. "He's upstairs," he told the crowd. One wonders how far upstairs he meant. In a death-denying culture, we vacillate between fear and fascination.

When my brother died, it was as if snow were falling all over the world; there is no silence as perfect as that of the shell-shocked bereaved trying to be brave. Kübler-Ross gave death and dying a language. She developed a series of seminars using interviews with terminal patients in which she encouraged physicians and others not to shy away from the sick but to get closer to them.

On the prairies, in winter, farmers have been known to tie a rope between the house and barn so they don't get lost in a blinding snowstorm. Kübler-Ross's model served as a kind of rope for the times when it seemed all landmarks were gone. She brought the subject out of the privacy of medical schools and delivered it to the streets. Death was out of the proverbial closet, so to speak. Her five stages of grief—denial, anger, bargaining, depression and acceptance—provided new ways to speak and think about loss, for the dying and for the bereaved. One of the misconceptions about this model is that one needs to reach acceptance in order to have a good death. In actual clinical practice, psychologist Therese Rando notes that true acceptance, as articulated by Kübler-Ross, is seldom witnessed. Rather, it appears that as patients get closer to death, the realization of the inevitable often provides a sense that "one's time has come" which, in some cases, allows the patient to make peace with the fact that there is nothing else to do. The line between acceptance and surrender is a very fine one. "I may not like this," one patient told me, "but the boat's leaving and I'm jumping on."

Not long ago, I met a family whose mother was dying of heart failure. Emotions were changing in the room like a spring day, with its hail one minute and sun the next. One daughter, at peace with her mother's dying in the morning, was bargaining with her to eat, in order to regain her strength, by early afternoon. A son who refused to accept that death was imminent, who had been in denial since his mother was admitted to hospital as a palliative patient, was the only one who answered his mother directly when she asked if she was dying. "Yes, Mom," he said, "you are in the hospital and you are dying." She responded by thanking him. "I'll miss you," she said, "I'll miss everything." She then closed her eyes and said, "Well, I'd better figure out how to do this, then."

There is no road map for the dying or the bereaved. No linear path. There are stages that go back and forth. Moments of grace, moments of anguish. Grief is a mess. Studies in medical anthropology have shown that death is defined as "good" if there is awareness, acceptance and preparation and a peaceful, dignified dying. We tame death with our ideas about it.

Historically, the good death, as established by religious doctrine, was one that was fully and consciously prepared for. In the Middle Ages, the dying organized their own bedside ceremonies, where friends and family gathered to eat, drink, play games and pray. The dying person expressed sorrow that life was coming to an end and spoke openly about his or her life, seeking forgiveness or forgiving others. The emphasis was on the soul's future. French historian Philippe Ariès referred to these ceremonies as "tame deaths." Ariès believed that when the bedside ceremonies were completed, and peace had been made, death was tamed because it was under God's control.

"In the twenty-first century," says Miriam, a hospice counsellor, "the good death, like the good birth, speaks to me about the need for control or a plan." A plan that, until fairly recently, many people believed was God's. Baby boomers may be, as a generation, the first group to face death without the structure or comfort of faith. Religious counsel has largely been replaced by secular grief counsellors who call upon the rhetoric of psychology and are parachuted in when tragedy strikes. Our grandparents trusted doctors: they were like priests. This was before Google turned us all into specialists. What does this mean for us? In the absence of faith, what do people want?

"No pain, no symptoms, mental clarity, choices around location, love, a big-screen TV, a death without lingering, death without ugliness," muses Miriam.

"What do they want?" she goes on. "A sense of humour, grace, profound final conversations, no final conversations, no death, to hear that it has all been a mistake, to be able to return to work, no service, no funeral. No place in the ground that will be a site of weeping and remembering. And, yet, to be remembered. Somehow.

"We're terrified," she says, "that we need to be our own specialists."

We know everything and nothing. We're terrified that no one really knows anything. It is hard to have a good death when one is in terror. I saw many good deaths in hospice, when both patients and their families were ready and death occurred gently, and I also met people who felt they were failing at their own deaths; some who didn't feel ready to die, others who felt frightened and unprepared.

There were many times I too felt frightened and unprepared in the face of a difficult death. Some deaths are tame, others are feral: wild and unpredictable. I felt helpless one evening when I was called to see a young woman who desperately did not want to die. Death, like birth, has a momentum of its own. Her breathing was rapid and shallow, like a woman in the transitional stage of labour. The only thing I could think to do was to match her breathing; a rhythm that, once started, brought back my own experience of birth. When my pain had been too intense, panting had helped to ease it. When I didn't think I could go on, focusing on the breath helped. As I slowed my breathing, she too slowed hers. I talked to her about breath and transition and the hard labour of dying; the language of birth was no different from the language of death. There had been no time to put a chair beside her bed; when I came into the room, I sat on the side of her bed. When she died, my face was inches from hers and her parents were each holding one of her hands.

With birth, we labour to bring a squalling baby into the room; what, then, I ask with no small amount of exasperation, do we labour for in our dying? This feels like a brainteaser, a thanatological Rubik's cube. Imagine three rooms: one we come from, one we live in and one we exit into. We labour to be born and we labour to die. We enter with our mother's hard work and exit with our own hard labour. The obvious analogy is the clichéd one: we come from the unknown and depart for the unknown. In between we dig ditches, build cities, plough fields; we toil under the midday sun and, exhausted, we share the fruits of our labour. Maybe, just maybe, what matters is not the purpose of the work, but the work itself.

Work through the morning hours, goes the old hymn, *work in the glowing sun. Work for the night is coming, when man's work is done.*

It can be a comfort for some families to think of dying as work. There is a purpose to work, an inherent self-sufficiency. If we can work, we can look after ourselves; there is a feeling that we are not completely helpless. Breath is crucial to both kinds of labour. Prenatal classes focus on breath and pain; the progression in Lamaze classes is from deep to shallow breathing. The dying, too, move from regular deep breaths to shallow mouth breathing. At the end, the dying often look like fish out of water, their mouths opening and closing in a kind of reflex. One could almost mistake these last breaths for silent kisses.

The sights and sounds shook me. There were nights, after a difficult shift, when I would take my clothes off and drop them outside the bedroom door. Nights I didn't want to touch my children, when I felt I carried death with me on my skin like a contagion. Once, after a visit at which the smell of death was too strong, the nurse I was with stopped the car and we got out and buried our faces in a lilac bush hanging over a white picket fence in a quiet neighbourhood where nobody needed us.

Everything we love, we must leave. How is it we are not inconsolable? Like water running or baby crying?

––––––––––––

Of the twelve principles for a good death identified by the authors of the British study *The Future of Health Care of Older People*, eight have to do with control—from the right to know when death is coming to retaining control of it when it happens. As much as we plan for death, there is something that escapes us, something we can't quite take in. "One of the main reasons it's so easy to march men off to war," says Ernest Becker, is that "each of them feels sorry for the man next to him who will die." Unlike lion tamer Clyde Beatty, who tamed his cats with a chair and a whip, we use our intellect to try to bargain with death, thinking we can make a deal, forgetting there is a wildness at the heart of it.

Some of us drink beer instead of hard liquor, or vow to smoke five cigarettes a day instead of twenty-five if only we can keep smoking; some, like the thirty-three Chilean miners hauled up out of a collapsed mine 2,300 feet deep in the Atacama Desert on August 5, 2010, after sixty-nine days underground, promise to give up mistresses and return to the Church as new and devoted men.

We forget, as Kay Ryan's poem "On the Nature of Understanding" shows us, how unpredictability is built into things:

Say you hoped to
tame something
wild and stayed
calm and inched up
day by day. Or even
not tame it but
meet it halfway.
Things went along.
You made progress,
understanding
it would be a
lengthy process,
sensing changes
in your hair and
nails. So it's
strange when it
attacks: you thought
you had a deal.

Within days of starting work at hospice, it became clear to me that what we hope to control and what we actually control are vastly different things. "We are most deeply asleep at the switch," writes Annie Dillard, "when we fancy we control any switches at all."

A man in the final stages of ALS reconnected with a daughter he had been estranged from for many years. Paralyzed from the neck down, he wanted to change his will to include his daughter, but his second wife did not want it changed and would not help him. The day before he died, four colleagues from work came to his house, carried him to the car and drove him to a lawyer, where he responded to questions by blinking his eyes and succeeded, in this way, in changing his will. He went into respiratory distress that evening and died shortly after being given enough morphine to feel that he wasn't suffocating to death. Our idea of control may undergo profound changes as we approach death. Václav Havel believed that hope was not the same thing as optimism. It was not, he believed, the conviction that something would turn out well; rather, it was "the certainty that something makes sense, regardless of how it turns out." In the end, what we control may be as minute as the blinking of an eye.

One night recently, Patrick and I curled up in bed and watched *Philadelphia* on my laptop. In the morning, he commented that the final scene, in which Tom Hanks lies dying of AIDS in a room full of family and friends, seemed like a portrayal of a good death. In 1993, when Jonathan Demme made the film, the disease was still a stigmatized illness. That same year, Russian ballet star Rudolf Nureyev, known to have AIDS, was said to have died of "cardiac problems." He was buried in his evening clothes with his medals and favourite beret.

In the mid- to late eighties, young men dying of AIDS radicalized the dying process. Their bedside ceremonies were secular incarnations of the tame deaths of the Middle Ages. AIDS activist David Lewis, a Vancouver psychologist who committed suicide in 1990, disclosed to a local newspaper that he had assisted in the deaths of eight of his friends who had the disease. Lewis's friends came when he decided it was time. One secured the Seconal that was needed; others sat with him, visiting, drinking a few beers and saying goodbye. A nurse set up the IV, but the suicide note left by Lewis was clear: it was he who had turned on the spigot releasing the drugs into his system. He died within the hour. For Lewis and his friends, death was a kind of final political act.

We want to believe in the good death. With all our hearts we want to believe in this.

Often, when death finally comes after a long illness, it is good simply because it is an end to suffering. I saw people who were ahead of their own deaths; people who were ready but whose bodies were not quite done. I saw families who said their goodbyes and then waited for what seemed like intolerable days of pointless suffering; people who questioned whether or not we were kinder to animals, by putting them out of their suffering, than we were to our own kind.

Joseph, a Baha'i, knocked on God's door every night. Too weak to get out of bed, each night he visualized himself standing in the doorway, calling into an empty room.

"Hello," he called out, "is anybody there?" All around him he could hear the scratchings and scrapings of ascension. Every night Joseph went to the door, and every morning he cried to find himself denied access.

The door of knowledge of the Ancient Being hath ever been and will continue to be closed in the face of man, decreed Baha'ullah. How fair is that? Joseph was ready to die two weeks before his body gave out.

It's a long walk we take at the end to meet our maker. You'd think someone would answer when we bang on the door.

––––––

In a visit reminiscent of the scene in which Tom Hanks, enraptured, listens to Maria Callas singing the aria "La Mamma Morta" from Umberto Giordano's opera *Andrea Chénier*, I met a thirty-year-old man dying of AIDS who was in his small rooftop garret listening to *The Four Seasons* by Vivaldi when I arrived. The volume was cranked as high as it could go and there was both a madness and an exquisite beauty to the violin's interpretation of "Winter." That's all I remember — sitting beside him, listening. Tears streaming down both our faces.

My nephew, Isaac, was born deaf. A few years before he died of AIDS, in his early twenties, I learned sign language so that I could speak with him. When I painstakingly spelt out my first greetings to him, he turned to his mom and signed, "Is there something wrong with my auntie?" My words, slowly and deliberately formed, hung in the air one silent letter at a time. The sign we both understood was the one he made for *crazy* as he kissed my cheek and took off out the door.

At Isaac's funeral, in a hall on the Burrard Reserve on Dollarton Highway, his father, Leonard — who had just finished a round of chemo for throat cancer — bent down low, spread his arms wide open and began, haltingly, to dance his son's eagle dance. It wasn't that he became an eagle that struck me so deeply, but that he remained a man, earthbound, limited, moving in sweeping circles around his youngest son's casket. Tilting towards earth the way the great birds do.

And what was it we wanted? To be remembered. Somehow.

Hope

Hope, writes Emily Dickinson, *is the thing with feathers that perches in the soul.*

This kind of hope makes us giddy. Our hearts somersault, we feel it in our bodies. This kind of hope is a bird: a quickening, a fluttering, we feel it in our chests. It lives inside us, a ruby-throated beauty. It flies and sings and, if shot down, plunges to the earth.

———————

To speak about hope can be tricky. We're told not to lose it, as if it were a thing we might misplace if we're not careful, like our passports or car keys. We're told we must have it and that we can't live without it and that it's still there even though we can't see it—like one's invisible childhood friend. Hope and prayer are often linked together. When faced with serious challenges, we might say, "I hope and pray" that things work out. Prayer, unlike hope, looks to a higher power to intervene. Hope is earthbound—a kind of secular prayer.

Recently, I read an article by Dr. Martin Scurr, medical columnist for the *Daily Mail*, in which he wrote, "Should I discover tomorrow that I have advanced, life-threatening cancer, I won't go rushing to the doctors for a heavily invasive course of medical treatment. No, I will shut up my London surgery, head to my home in Norfolk, stock up on gin and tonic and have a jolly good time until I meet my end." Doctors, it seems, base their hope on what they've seen; they know enough about modern medicine to know its limits. The rest of us are often unsure what to base our hopes on. A fine Scotch whisky, I think, is a good start.

The language of terminal illness is characterized by hopelessness. There is nothing left to do, there is no hope for a cure; It's hopeless, people think and are often told. What I found, over time, was that hope changes. Sometimes meaning is found in the last weeks moving slowly towards death—in a reconciliation or an opportunity to speak about things not spoken about before; in celebrating a last birthday or the birth of a child. We are hard-wired for hope. Illness itself is hope's alchemist. At the beginning, with the initial diagnosis, the hope is for a cure; over time, as the person loses any quality of life—when they're unresponsive or in intractable pain—the hope may be for an end to suffering.

Viktor Frankl believed it was possible to find ways to create meaning out of suffering. Meaning is not something handed down from God, in Frankl's opinion; rather, it is to be found in our own human responses to tragedy. When a good friend of my daughter's died attempting to rescue a kayaker caught in a whirlpool, his family was devastated but found some solace in the fact that he died trying to save a life. Families of accident victims may find a measure of comfort if their loved one's organs can be used; sometimes people fight to have laws enacted—to toughen drunk-driving penalties, for instance—or create scholarships in the name of the deceased. We look for meaning; our hope is that our loved one did not die in vain.

From the Old English *hopian*, meaning "to wish, expect, look forward to something," hope allows us to imagine a future. On the other hand, if we're not careful, if we're too focused on what we want to happen, we can miss what is happening right in front of us. Hope can be a thief. It can steal the present moment right out from under our feet.

Species Song

In the preface to her book *Hologram*, P. K. Page explores the relationship between voice and influence. In trying to understand how poets come to sing their own unique songs, she came across a report by an ornithologist who raised songbirds in isolation in order to understand how they learned to sing. Removed from their nests before ever hearing a note, the birds cobbled together a kind of song; not species perfect, but a song nonetheless. When introduced to the songs of other birds, not of their own species, he discovered that they chose the notes and cadences that completed their own species song.

"Of course," she thought, "that is what poets do. We have a song—of a kind. But it is not until we have heard many other songs that we are able to put together our own specific song."

I came to hospice without the framework that established beliefs offer. God was a benign presence in the house I grew up in; my mother believed in some kind of afterlife, although she couldn't say what. I'm still not sure, when I pray, whom or what I pray to.

I know very little of my Jewish ancestry since that lineage is on my father's side and Jewish identity is passed through matrilineal descent. From Baghdad to Russia to Calcutta and Shanghai and on to Israel, my ancestors studied Kabbalah and steeped themselves in Jewish and Arabic philosophy; they were Levys and Cohens and had names such as Seema, Mozelle, Solomon and Dafna. Still, I do not qualify as a Jew. On the other hand, my former marriage to a Coast Salish man made me legally an Indian under section 12(1)(b) of the Indian Act. I am at home in the longhouse and a stranger in the synagogue.

Within Salish culture there is a familiarity with death based on an extensive history of loss. The dead are said to walk amongst the living and children are told not to eat outside after three p.m., as the ghosts are hungry and lonely for human company. Death is no stranger. Sometimes he appears as a man in a long black overcoat sitting in the branches of a tree swinging his feet. Sometimes he disguises himself as a bird. Sometimes there is a sign. On the night my father-in-law died, a high wind howled around our house, causing the lights to flicker on and off. At the same time, a thousand miles away in San Diego, the lights flickered in his eldest daughter's house.

I was intrigued by what I often saw as a practical response to problems of the spirit in Salish culture. On the West Coast, fire is a conduit between worlds. Among all phenomena, said French philosopher Gaston Bachelard, fire is the only one that can be so definitely attributed to the opposing forces of good and evil. "It shines in Paradise. It burns in Hell. It is a pleasure for the good child sitting prudently in front of the hearth; yet it punishes disobedience when the child wishes to play too close to its flames." The Egyptians believed it to be an insatiable animal, Persians made sacrifices to it; at the beginning of astronomical study, people of the Middle Ages thought that fire was in fact food for the stars. Prometheus stole it from Zeus and returned it to mankind; a Salish legend tells how Beaver and Woodpecker stole fire from the Salmon and gave it to the ghosts.

When my father-in-law died, we burned his favourite armchair, along with a gallon of Calona Red and his sharpest carving knife, so that he could feel at ease in his new home. I stood in the backyard of his house at the foot of the Chief Mountain and watched as the flames consumed the chair in minutes, leaving the blackened springs like the carcass of a beached whale. My father-in-law drank himself to death; I remember thinking how amazing it was that his wife put a gallon of rotgut wine on the burn pile for him. The ceremonies are non-judgmental: if the deceased drank himself to death with cheap wine, then cheap wine will be on the table.

I was drawn instinctively to many of these Salish rituals and practices. It made sense to light a candle in order to hold the spirit in the last days and hours; it made sense that someone should sit with the body from the time of death until burial or cremation so that the spirit would not feel frightened or abandoned; it seemed right to pick up a handful of dirt and throw it on the coffin before the plot was filled in—"a last handshake," as the Coast Salish call it.

What I didn't know, and was stunned to find out one afternoon, reading *Kaddish* by Leon Wieseltier on the steps of King's College in London, Ontario, was that the Native rituals that had resonated most deeply with me were also the rituals and beliefs of Jewish culture. Whereas the Salish light candles to hold the spirit of the dead, so Jewish tradition directs that a candle will burn for seven days to guide the soul from this earth to the next; whereas the mirrors are covered in Salish homes to protect the living from the gaze of the dead, mirrors are covered in Jewish homes to remind the mourners that this is a time to focus not on themselves but on the dead. In both traditions, from the moment of death, the body is not left alone until burial. Within the Jewish tradition, the people who sit with the dead body are called *shomrim*; within Salish culture, a watchman volunteers to sit the night through.

"Tradition is not reproduced. It is thrown and caught," says Wieseltier. "It lives a long time in the air."

From lighting candles and sitting with the body, to covering mirrors and throwing dirt in the grave—I had unwittingly been learning my own species song.

Test Pilots

I was regularly asked, by family members, to describe the dying process. I would tell them about how people often lapse into a coma in the days preceding death and how breath moves from the deep and regular to the shallow and intermittent. I would explain apnea and how people often hold their breath for long periods of time, up to three minutes sometimes, and how everyone in the room also holds their breath until the gasping breath breaks the silence in the room. I would explain that people rarely die in the space between breaths, that they return to the body as if they've been on a practice run.

I would go over the possibility that phlegm would build up, resulting in what is known as a *death rattle*, a term that evokes a kind of dread, a term that conjures up scenes like the one Dostoevsky describes in *Crime and Punishment*: "She sank more and more into uneasy delirium. At times she shuddered, turned her eyes from side to side, recognized everyone for a minute, but at once sank into delirium again. Her breathing was hoarse and difficult; there was a sort of rattle in her throat." I would talk about how the hands and feet get cold as blood leaves the extremities and pools around the heart and lungs in a last attempt to protect the vital organs, and how those hands and feet turn blue shortly before death. And I would talk about how the breath leaves the body, how it moves from the chest to the throat to the last little fish breaths.

The human embryonic heart starts beating approximately three weeks after conception: we are older than our hearts by twenty-one days. In the end, however, our hearts often outlive us, firing on for seconds, sometimes minutes, after our last breath. The moment of death is not always immediately evident; defining death has become a complicated business. In cases of brain death, ventilators, puffing like bike pumps, keep people alive after they have been declared legally dead, so that their organs can be harvested—not unlike a scene from the 1978 film *Coma* with Geneviève Bujold. In ICUs, bodies are attached to machines that beep and chime with blue, green and red lines marking blood pressure, oxygen and heart rate on monitors that look like weather maps tracking massive storms.

"The proof that we don't understand death," says Jerry Seinfeld, "is that we give dead people a pillow."

When writer Eleanor Vincent's nineteen-year-old daughter was thrown from a horse and declared legally brain-dead twenty years ago, she was kept alive for a brief period so that her organs could be used. Eleanor remembers saying her final goodbye: "I learned that my daughter's brainstem was actually gangrenous at the time she was declared legally dead. There was no chance she could ever live. Nonetheless, she appeared alive with rosy cheeks and a rising and falling chest when I stood before her for the last time." In many ways, writes Vincent, "technology has fully outstripped our ability to comprehend what death is."

With medical advances, we are faced with complex decisions about death—our own and those of our loved ones— in ICUs, hospital wards and hospices. When do we stop chemo, radiation, dialysis, surgery? At what point do we sign a do-not-resuscitate order letting people know that we do not want our ribs broken in an attempt to jump-start the heart? Keeping people alive in order to use their organs blurs the margin between life and death. Where is the demarcation line? In the words of bioethicist Stuart Youngner, "You could say, well, they're almost dead, or they're close to dead or they're dead enough."

That's it, I think, *when they're dead enough* and not a moment before.

At a recent dinner party, a friend talked about how, when the undertakers came shortly after her mother's death to take the body away, her five-year-old daughter protested, saying, "It's too soon, she needs time to rest from dying." What's the rush? We need time: the dead, the living, the nearly dead, the newly dead. Send the experts away; we all just need to think like five-year-olds. For a little while, anyway.

In his memoir *Patrimony*, Philip Roth writes about how, when his father was critically ill, he decided, along with the doctor, to forgo heroics and let his father die a natural death. The doctor, who was prepared to put Roth's elderly father on life support, explained that once the ventilator was connected, it could not legally be disconnected. Roth leaned in close to his father and whispered, "Dad, I'm going to have to let you go." A phrase he kept repeating until, as he says in the book, "I believed it myself." Once, the Grim Reaper called the shots — and ultimately he still does — but death's timetable has been co-opted by modern medicine.

Statistically, we are more likely to die at night when metabolic activity is at its lowest. The numbers also show we're more likely to die of heart attacks on Monday mornings and, if we're in hospital, weekends are a risky business. In my experience, people often died around five a.m. Once, when I was called around that time of the morning and told that a fifteen-year-old girl had died of lupus, I asked my ex-husband, as I headed out the door to meet the girl's mother, what I could possibly say to her. I knew of her daughter; I knew that, after she was diagnosed at ten years old, she had slept in her mother's bed every night and that they were inseparable. "Tell her that the heavens open at five a.m.," he said. "Tell her that is when the souls are gathered up and welcomed home with wide-open arms." I was unsure about sharing this, not wanting to impose or make things "right" too easily, but as I sat with her and waited for the funeral home to come, I mentioned it and for the briefest of moments I thought I saw something like relief cross her face.

The idea of "home" is compelling. Pacific salmon are unique in that spawning is the last act of their life cycle. Hell-bent for home, after years at sea, they return to lay their eggs and die in the streams and rivers where they were born. In Goldstream Park, not far from where I live, the salmon start appearing around mid-October. A few years ago, after a hot summer, I watched the fish thrash their way over dry rocks to reach a trickle of water, where they rested before jackknifing themselves into pools no deeper than two inches.

The instinct for home is a powerful one.

The dying, too, are often hell-bent for home. For the devout, it may mean going home to God; for the secular, it may have more to do with riverbeds and the urge to return to the original source. When they talk about wanting to go home, it is up to the living to decipher what this means. Sometimes it is a physical place: they want to leave the hospital and go home to die. Other times it is metaphorical. One man I met told his family on a Monday that he was going home at 3:18 p.m. on Thursday. Everyone, including me, waited to see what would happen. Thursday came and went, and we all felt a bit foolish for having thought we were witnessing an astonishing prediction. Who is to say the dying are punctual? He died the following day at precisely 3:18.

———

People want to know if the dying can hear at the end. I once listened to an ICU intensivist talk to a family whose mother was in a coma.

"Can she hear us?" they asked.

"Yes," he replied. "She hears you the way a newborn hears the sound of its mother's voice."

I immediately liked that description. We hear our mother's voices in utero; we hear them when we're lying in our cradles and buggies. Before comprehension, there is comfort in the rise and fall of the familiar; words are less important than presence; meaning gives way to music and comfort.

My friend Lorna cites her love of Barry Manilow as a kind of proof of the subterranean existence of hearing—proof that the dying in a non-responsive state can hear us when we speak to them. When she comes home from a night shift at the hospital, she puts on her headphones and drifts off to the sounds of the local radio station. Nothing disturbs her: not the kids getting ready for school, the dog barking, not the garbage truck rumbling down the street. The only thing that can pull her out of sleep, she says, is if a Manilow song comes on the radio. She is unfazed by my clear ridicule of her musical tastes. Finishing off her tea, she smiles when she looks at me. "Proof," is all she says.

"Music began," says the British artist and writer John Berger, "with a howl lamenting a loss. The howl became a prayer and from the hope in the prayer started music, which can never forget its origin. In it, hope and loss are a pair."

What, then, do the dying hear when we stand and wail at their bedsides? A sound more Wagnerian than Brahmsian? More Sturm und Drang than lullaby? In the longhouse each winter, the new dancers can be heard crying from their make-shift tents on the bleachers above the dirt floor. Over a period of four days the dancers, known as babies, receive a song and a spirit helper during their initiation as spirit dancers. The drummers, listening carefully, circle the baby whose cry seems most urgent and begin to drum and sing in time with each cry. They know the beginnings of the dancers' spirit songs are in their inconsolable wails. There are moments when I wonder if the dying might hear, in the cries of the grief-stricken, the first notes of their own songs.

In the early 1950s, child psychiatrist John Bowlby developed a theory of attachment. He believed the cries of a child served to reunite the infant with the mother; when the baby cries, the mom comes running. In grief, his theory holds: adults are all like children seeking reunion with the deceased. We wail to call them back. We wail so the bond won't be broken. We wail with incomprehension at the separation. The truths are contradictory. When I first began working with the dying, I was struck by the resounding silence on the unit. In a place where people were dying every day, patients rarely cried and family members did not wail in corridors. Nobody tore their clothes or shook their fists at God. It was as if death itself was sleeping in the dimly lit rooms and nobody wanted to disturb it.

The polite silence wasn't what I expected; but then, what did I expect? Something more Dionysian than Apollonian: more wine and drunkenness than cool marble and contemplation. Some sound to rise from the belly of grief. A howl and a respondent howl across a frozen lake. Something.

Go to the Health and Wellness section of most bookstores and you will find titles such as *Dying Beautifully*, *Messages from the Light*, *Perfect Endings*, *Peaceful Dying* and *Deathing: An Intelligent Alternative for the Final Moments of Life*. Death is marketed as a teachable moment, a New Age journey for the enlightened. Take another look and you'll often see the section right beside the one on death is stacked with books on sexuality. *La petite mort*, the French say for orgasm. Our ambivalence is clearly on display: we have one foot in the fire, the other in the grave. In North America it is easier to talk about sex than death. In the past, it was acceptable to talk to children about death but not sex; they were included at the deathbed at the same time as being told they were brought by the stork. Today, they receive sex education at school but might be told their loved ones are now stars twinkling in the heavens.

Sometimes we need help to break through our decorum. In many parts of the world, professionals are hired to cry at funerals. Wailers, usually women, stand by the grave and openly grieve; their high cries, a kind of ululation, spread amongst the mourners until they too break down. In Chile they were called *lloronas*; in Malaysia and Singapore in the 1960s it was said there were so many paid mourners at funerals it was hard to know if the families were actually there. In ancient Egypt, women were hired to cry and beat their breasts as it was believed the dead were ready to avenge the slightest sign of indifference on the part of those left behind. When I was ten, in grade five, I was assigned the role of grieving widow in a play we were performing about an Irish fisherman lost at sea. "You must keen," said Mrs. Black, referring to the Irish word *caoinim*, meaning "to weep, wail, lament."

Every day I stood on imaginary cliffs above the crashing waves and wailed as if my heart were breaking and my teacher had to gently suggest I tone it down just a little bit.

The poet Stanley Kunitz believed that all one's feelings about death are a kind of elegy for the erotic. A lament for the carnal, from the Latin *carnis*, pertaining to the body and its appetites. *Desire*, he says, is one of the strongest words in the language. What makes the engine go? asks Kunitz.

> *Desire, desire, desire.*
> *The longing for the dance*
> *stirs in the buried life.*
> *One season only,*
> *and it's done.*
> *So let the battered old willow*
> *thrash against the windowpanes*
> *and the house timbers creak.*
> *Darling, do you remember*
> *the man you married? Touch me,*
> *remind me who I am.*

The flame guttering still throws an exquisite heat. Eros helps the soul to remember beauty. The simplest things look dazzling when we fall in love; time is altered, the world looks new. All the clichés are true. At the same time, falling in love does not banish thoughts of death; if anything, it makes thoughts of death more frequent. How, we wonder, will we survive if something happens to our beloved?

If eros helps the soul to remember beauty, dying can show us beauty as if for the first time. A colleague dying of breast cancer in her mid-thirties pointed to the things in her room—books, photographs of her lover, her worn leather jacket swung over the back of a chair, her journal on the kitchen table open to the page she was working on, her cat, light streaming in through the window—and asked "How do I leave this? How do I say goodbye?"

What, I wonder, did my brother love? To what would he have said goodbye?

In the end, we breathe from our reptilian brain, the part of the brain possessed by the reptiles that preceded mammals roughly 200 million years ago. Breathing, heart rate and the fight-or-flight mechanism are controlled by the part of our brains also found in lizards, crocodiles and birds. The impulses of the brain stem, lacking language, are instinctual and ritualistic. During the process of natural death, the reptilian brain guides the body through the complex process of shutting down, turning out the lights, slowing down the lungs until the last breath is taken.

It has been noted that when mountain climbers are in danger of falling, this brain takes over; the eyesight intensifies and the feet miraculously take the right steps. Could it be that our reptilian brains help us to step miraculously towards our deaths? The American neurologist Paul MacLean theorizes that we have not one brain but three: the reptilian brain, symbolized by cold; the mammalian brain, by warmth; and the new brain, whose symbol is light. The gold light around Buddha's head in statues is an attempt to show he is living in his new brain. Some Tibetan meditators of the thirteenth century, says Robert Bly, were able to read in the dark by the light given off from their own bodies.

It is not uncommon for there to be periods of agitation shortly before death. People often try to rise from their beds as if they have to get somewhere. When they are too weak to get up, they might reach with their arms towards something only they can see, pinching their index finger and thumb together repeatedly in an effort to catch whatever is floating by them. In clinical terms, it is known as pre-death restlessness and is diagnosed by the medical profession as a kind of delirium brought about by physical changes. When my friend's husband was close to death, he pumped his arms as if about to fly. Some doctors differentiate toxic delirium, an altered state caused by pain medication and other drugs, from terminal delirium, which is seen as part of the dying process. Either way, the medical profession sees delirium as a physiological problem possibly caused by some unknown source such as dehydration, electrolyte imbalance or the release of endorphins or other brain chemicals shortly before death.

I'm not so sure.

Over time, it began to appear to me as if the dying were venturing out on a kind of test flight; as if they were working hard to figure out how to leave the body. Episodes of agitation were offset by periods of deep stillness, periods in which family members would comment that it felt as if their loved one was not there. It was as if the silver cord, in the book of Ecclesiastes, binding the spirit to the body, were stretching farther and farther until it finally snapped. Other than *The Tibetan Book of Living and Dying*, there are few manuals on how to leave the body—the container that houses all that we are; it's up to each of us to figure it out. "How," one man asked, "will I know that I am dead?"

Imagine the dying as test pilots: figuring out ways to best recover from spins, breaking the sound barrier, flying straight towards the sun, bailing out when the plane is going down.

Of course, things don't always go as planned. One afternoon I went with a nurse to the home of a man who was extremely restless. As much as possible, a nurse and a counsellor work together on the palliative response team so that the counsellor can attend to any emotional and practical needs while the nurse deals with the immediate medical crisis. We parked in front of his house and walked up the sidewalk to the door. There were roses growing beneath the bay window on our right and we could see the man attempting to climb out of his hospital bed on the other side of the window. His wife, who had not slept for days, was beside herself. While the nurse drew up a syringe of Haldol, I spoke gently with the man.

"You can rest now," I said. "You can rest."

He looked at me and lay very still. His wife, overjoyed, couldn't thank me enough. I felt good, even a bit smug, until he motioned his wife over.

"Call our lawyer," he said.

"Why?" she wondered.

"Because," he said, pointing directly at me, "that woman just arrested me."

Whatever works, I thought to myself, whatever works.

Morphine sometimes causes delusions. One woman saw spiders hanging from the ceiling of her room at hospice. Some of them dropped down on her bed and crawled over her face when she was sleeping. She was terrified to close her eyes. People talked to her, telling her there were no spiders, the doctors changed her medication, but she didn't believe anyone. In the end, the only thing that helped was to pack up her belongings and move her to a different room, where she settled in and never saw the imaginary spiders on their imaginary webs ever again. When Muhammad called the mountain to him, it didn't budge. "Well then," he said, "if the mountain won't come to Muhammad, then Muhammad must go to the mountain." There are times you just have to act. Simple as that.

To the Western mind, waking hallucinations about the dead are considered delusional projections of the living—dismissed as indicative of wishful thinking or as evidence of denial or craziness. The one exception to this line of thought is found in studies on widowhood, which reveal that human attachment bonds often persist beyond death. It is not uncommon for widows to have a sense of continued contact with their spouses, including a sense of presence and touch. The dying, too, often talk about sensing the presence of the dead. Sometimes it's a smell, a certain perfume or cologne; sometimes they hear them speaking. One woman asked me to pull up a chair beside her bed so that her late mother could have a seat; another stared at the left-hand corner of her room for days, waiting for her late husband to return for her; others came, she told us, but she didn't know them and refused to go. On the morning of her death, she said her husband had come. He'd tipped his hat in the slightly mocking way he'd always done, and she smiled. A wide, radiant smile.

I DID NOT SET OUT TO RETRIEVE MY BROTHER OR ASSUAGE AN OLD grief when I began writing about death, and yet it seems he keeps serendipitously finding me.

When I first visited his grave, with my mother and sister, thirty years after his death, the unmistakable smell of cigarette smoke flooded the car when I parked. None of us smoked, and when I got out of the car and looked around, there were no discarded butts to be seen. I asked my sister if Ian smoked. "Like a chimney," she said. I have no way of knowing if he was there, no way to discern between wishful thinking and a spiritual encounter, but as we started down the hill, I thought I could see him, clear as day, sitting on the rock wall, swinging his feet. Saying, "It's damned well about time."

My mother, sister and I arrived at the cemetery only to find it had just been mowed; all the flat headstones were covered in grass and impossible to read. My mother, who had attended the burial in a state of profound grief, had no idea where to start looking and began slowly walking amongst the graves. My sister, Carol, and I took off down the hill to see if there was any logic to how the plots were arranged, only to find there were no clues: old graves and new graves were side by side. Unable to go any further, my mother half collapsed on a red bench streaked with the evidence of recent bird strikes. "None of my deaths have markers," she told me when I went to sit with her and put my arm around her shoulders.

A few minutes later, Carol, who had been futilely kicking the grass off concrete slabs, walked slightly to the right of the bench and suddenly stopped, threw up her arms and exclaimed, "Here he is!" I don't know if we found him or he found us. It doesn't matter. Between the three of us that day, our offerings included a handful of lily of the valley from Mom's garden, an empty coffee cup to put them in, and a pencil that my sister tucked in the thin edge between the stone marker and the grass. "My brother," she said, "never went anywhere without a pencil." In a sea of green, our mother had sat down right in front of her son.

At a recent writers' festival on Galiano Island, one of the hundreds of islands and islets that form part of a larger archipelago in the southern part of the Salish Sea, the talk turned, as it often does with a group of writers, towards death. In the course of the conversation, in which I spoke about my brother, the novelist Audrey Thomas said that she had been at UBC in 1964 and had known Ian. They were both enrolled in an Anglo-Saxon seminar, and they met in Meredith Thompson's small office to translate Beowulf. She recalled how he would arrive in class, often hungover, and lean back on his chair, balancing on its two rear legs, and how she would wait to see if he would tumble backwards.

I like that; it seems accurate. I can see him precariously balanced. Between drink and study, recklessness and scholarship, between Angleterre and the New World. Between Here and There.

In a recent email, Audrey asked me if my brother, dead, had had a profound influence on my life. No, I think to myself, it is not the fact of Ian dead that shaped me; rather, it was his death. The sudden absence, the depth of silence, the inexplicable disappearance.

When Odysseus tries to embrace his mother in the under-world, she flutters out of his hands like a shadow and says to him,

> Sinews no longer bind the flesh and bones together—
> fire in all its fury burns the body to ashes
> and once life slips from the white bones, spirit,
> dreamlike, dissolves into the shadows.

All over the world, every second of every day, the dead are fluttering, like shadows, out of our hands.

Beliefs

In our encounters with the dying, we each bring our own beliefs—beliefs based on our history with death, our culture, religion or lack of it; beliefs based on mythology and psychology and on our motives and expectations. Our beliefs are a kind of architecture of the mind, a way of creating meaning and interpreting the world. In Africa, a widow might run a zigzag course through the woods after her husband's burial so that his ghost will not follow and haunt her. There are Japanese people who believe the dead arrive on the back of a horse on New Year's Day; when the holiday is over, they return them to their world in small wood and paper boats bearing lighted candles.

The Aztecs, Babylonians and Assyrians believed that all good people metamorphosed into birds, while ancient Egyptians believed that the soul, the *ba*, could leave the dead body in the form of a hawk. They built their graves and tombs with narrow shafts leading to the open air so that these birds could fly in and out, keeping watch over the body.

We acquire our beliefs as we go along, influenced by the tangible as well as the intangible. The beliefs I held about death as a child were influenced by fairy tales and prayers; a single kiss had the power to undo spells and restore life. At night, I knelt down beside my bed and recited "Now I Lay Me Down to Sleep." It had a nursery rhyme quality, four lyrical lines a child could easily memorize. Each night I prayed, *If I should die before I wake, I pray for God my soul to take*. Death winked at me before I knew what it was. Falling asleep felt a bit like coming unmoored—the frayed rope, holding the little boat, unravelling.

I grew up in a house of superstitions. Paintings falling off the walls or robins flying into the house meant a death would surely follow. My mother believed, with complete certainty, that crows were harbingers, and in our house, strangely, that seemed to be the case. I remember her screams one morning when a crow fell down the chimney, and the phone rang shortly afterwards to inform her of the murder of a close friend's daughter. After that, she warred with any crow that came close to the house—shaking her fists at the ones who squawked at her from the telephone lines.

"Don't be hanging around here, you bloody bastards," she'd yell out the kitchen window at six a.m.

––––––––

In the fifteenth century, the art of dying was laid out in the *Ars Moriendi*. A good Christian death, as prescribed in the two Latin texts, involved departing in a state of grace, denouncing Satan, praying to God, repenting one's sins, and—for Roman Catholics—receiving the sacraments. The *Ars Moriendi* survives in two different versions. The first is a longer treatise of six chapters that prescribes rites and prayers to be used at the time of death. The second is a brief illustrated book that shows the dying person's struggle with temptations before attaining a good death. In one of the illustrations, the Devil, pictured with a hooking staff, and Death himself, with a lance, are seen trying to snare the soul of a dying man while an angel hovers at the head of the bed. In another, demons crowd around a bed offering crowns to a skeletal figure who looks as though he has died of fright. The art of dying, in the fifteenth century, was not for the faint of heart.

The battle for our souls is no longer played out the way it was in the fifteenth century. What, I wonder, is the *Ars Moriendi* of our time? Whereas in the past we turned to priests or holy men, we now look to doctors for miraculous cures and extended lives. And yet we often pray for some kind of divine intervention even when we're not sure what or whom we believe in. There is a fundamental difference between saying "I'll pray for you" as opposed to "You're in my thoughts" or "I'm sending you love."

Religions point to the realm of the supernatural, assuring people they are not alone in the world, and yet, in an increasingly secular society, how do you bring people to God? "Through parking and bathrooms," says Scott Weatherford, lead pastor of Calgary's First Alliance Church. Weekend services in the church are high-tech multimedia spectacles with rock bands, big-screen monitors and fair-trade coffee, and a cupholder in every one of the 1,704 seats. It is harder to pull people in these days without a gimmick. Harder to believe in a God who, as one young pastor says, causes a place to boom economically in order "to do the good in the world that needs doing." In this case, that would place God smack dab up to his elbows in the black gold of the Alberta tar sands.

In the twenty-first century, how would we illustrate the art of dying? Gone would be the Devil with his hook, Death with his lance, the angel at the head of the bed. Replace the cot with a hospital bed, the angel with a doctor in scrubs, and put the Devil in charge of the IVs, heart monitors, ventilators, catheters, bags of blood and canisters of oxygen. As for Death himself, look as you will, he's nowhere to be seen. Of course, if all this talk of devils and demons is too much, you can dab—on your wrists and behind your ears—Ars Moriendi, a perfume oil made in California's Black Phoenix Alchemy Lab, whose most popular blends are Dance of Death, Darkness and Les Fleurs du Mal.

Many of the people I met were dying without the structure or comfort of traditional belief; it was no longer clear exactly what life after death might look like. The promise of an afterlife brings peace to some, but it is also fraught with many uncertainties. For Catholics, the souls of the dead spend time in purgatory until fully cleansed of imperfections. Limbo, derived from the Latin *limbus*, meaning "hem" or "border," is the region on the border of hell reserved for pre-Christian saints and unbaptized babies. Members of the Church of Jesus Christ of Latter-day Saints believe that heaven is divided into three separate kingdoms of glory: the celestial, the terrestrial and the telestial. The celestial kingdom is reserved for married Mormon couples who are on their way to becoming gods and goddesses; the terrestrial kingdom is for honourable people who have allowed themselves to become blinded by the wickedness of the world; and the telestial kingdom exists solely for liars, adulterers, murderers, thieves and whoremongers. Salvation, according to the Quran, depends on a man's actions and attitudes on earth. The afterworld is a place of reckoning. It is the promised land and the place where we will be judged.

Sometimes it isn't death we fear, but something else. Once, upon returning from a community visit, I was met at the elevator by a nurse who said there was a patient who was very distressed and wanted to know what it was like to die. "I told him that you would tell him," she said.

Right, I thought.

When I went to his room, Alistair was nodding off in a recliner with a glass of Scotch in his hand. "So," he said, opening his eyes, "you are the one who's going to tell me what it's like to die?"

All the things I had thought about saying on my walk down the hall to his room flew out the window. "No," I said, "I don't have a clue. You need to tell me."

Alistair took a long drink, and for the next two hours he talked and I listened. He talked about his fear that he had not been a good enough man and that, if there was someone on gatekeeping duty in the heavens, he would have a lot to answer for. At one point, motioning to a vase of slender purple irises on his dresser, he said, "Death has been sitting there for three nights, and tonight I think we'll sleep together."

"God is, or He is not," wrote Blaise Pascal in the seventeenth century. But which side to choose? His wager, as it was known, went something like this: weigh the gain and the loss in wagering that God is. . . . If you gain, you gain all; if you lose, you lose nothing. Wager, then, without hesitation that He is. Heads or tails. In the end, maybe it doesn't matter so much what we believe.

Danish physicist and Nobelist Niels Bohr once hung a horseshoe over his doorway. Appalled friends exclaimed that surely he didn't put any trust in such pathetic superstition. "No, I don't," he replied with composure, "but apparently it works whether you believe in it or not."

I believe it would be a fine thing to leave the world in a small wood and paper boat holding a lighted candle.

What belief—or perhaps instinct—compels the living to carry the dead out into the sun? Out of darkness into the light. A woman I met, whose premature baby had spent her short life in the intensive care unit, wanted her to feel the sun, wind, rain on her face. She wanted her to breathe air that didn't come from a plastic tube and to see something other than a fluorescent sun. When it became evident that her baby was going to die, the doctor agreed to take her off life support and bag her—give her oxygen by hand—until she was out of the hospital.

A strange cortège of nurses, family and friends walked in single file behind the doctor through the corridors. It was April. Winter and spring were doing their dance. When we came out the back door, it was raining. By the time we had walked across the parking lot and made our way to a nearby grassy hill, the sun was shining.

The baby's grandfather took up his drum and sang a song to her. She breathed on her own for a good five minutes. When she took her last breath, a single clap of thunder reverberated across the sky.

Her grandfather believed the clap of thunder meant the Creator had opened the heavens, swooped down, picked the baby up in his arms and booted it right on back to heaven.

My childhood world was filled with presences: fairies in the garden, water-babies beneath the lily pads in sunken barrels, birds that portended disaster the way the black clouds rolling in off the North Shore Mountains signalled rain. I was predisposed to believe in spirits; when you spend time around the dying, it is almost impossible not to believe in something. For most people I met, it was not Jesus or Allah who appeared in the days and hours before death; rather, it was a husband or lover, a long-lost mother, a wife, a child. Sometimes they appeared in dreams; other times the dying would just point at something nobody else could see. Quite often the dead would appear days before death and set up camp in the room.

I don't see spirits. But once, years ago, when I was eight months pregnant, I heard singing and drumming coming from the site of a Shaker church that had burnt to the ground years before. My mother-in-law said spirits were singing to welcome the baby, but I was never sure what I'd heard or whether I had really heard anything at all.

Since the 1960s, there has been a shift from "dwelling" to "seeking." We spend less time contemplating God than we do pursuing self-enlightenment, identifying ourselves as "spiritual" more than "religious." Many hospices have spiritual care coordinators responsible for "matters of the spirit." Inner experience has come to take precedence over creeds and congregations; we are encouraged to look within to find our spiritual selves as opposed to searching the starry heavens for evidence of our maker. If religion serves to calm our fears about the void and to explain where we go when we disappear, contemporary spirituality is defined by possibility over certainty. For most of the people I met, the afterlife was an unanswered question. Before 1971, less than 1 percent of Canadians ticked the "no religion" box on national surveys. Two generations later, writes Michael Valpy in the *Globe and Mail*, 23 percent, or nearly a quarter of the population, say they aren't religious. Overall, we now die with less certainty about where we're going than we did in the past; and it seems more of us are dying certain in our belief that there is nothing.

From the beginning of time, we have looked to mythology, philosophy, religion and science to explain to ourselves what happens after death. As narratives, they deal with the known, the unknown and the unknowable. It is the unknowable that sometimes gives me pause, that makes me wonder.

In the mid-1990s, I met a woman in her late thirties who was dying of lung cancer. She and her partner of ten years married on a West Coast beach a few months before her death. When asked if she wanted her ashes scattered on the same beach, she shot back, "I never double-book." She was funny and brilliant, and after she died, her husband appeared to go into a grief-induced psychosis. In the oldest story in the world, Gilgamesh cries out when his beloved friend Enkidu dies,

> *May the bear, the hyena, the panther mourn you,*
> *may the leopard, stag, lion—all creatures*
> *of the plains mourn you.*
> *As long as I have breath I will cry out*
> *like one who has lost her beloved.*

After the woman's body was removed from their home, her husband called to her from where he was lying on the couch. He asked her what she wanted for dinner and if she thought he needed a haircut. He didn't hear his children talking to him or his dad trying to tell him that she was gone.

A few days later, he didn't see me when I sat with him at the kitchen table as he began to write the eulogy that he was to deliver later that afternoon in the university chapel. He picked up a pen and began to write on a white sheet, pausing every so often to tilt his head as if listening intently. "What's that?" he'd say. "Of course I included that." And later, laughing as he erased a word he had just written, "Okay, okay, you were always the best speller." He would pause and then go on. "Thanks," he said at one point, "I'd forgotten that." It dawned on me as I watched him, hunched over the table, that he was listening to his wife and recording what he heard. His wife was writing her own eulogy.

I didn't feel her there; she wasn't there for me. I saw a man talking to a ghost. The thought briefly occurred to me, no doubt from watching *Casper the Friendly Ghost*, to throw flour in the air to see if an outline of a person would emerge out of the drifting white powder. It was at moments like these that I wondered if there was more, if life or consciousness somehow continues, even briefly. Of course, no shape materialized and the eulogy, when delivered by her husband that afternoon, was brilliant and funny and not even close to being "proof" of anything. But still, I wonder what it was I saw that morning.

At its most intense, grief is a kind of madness. We want everything—the bear, the hyena, the panther, strangers on the street, the world itself—to mourn with us. It is impossible to comprehend the separation; grief puts the griever in an altered state. The bereaved walk the halls at night, sometimes they stop eating, they withdraw from the world and search for their beloved in places they used to go together;

they rip their clothes and pull out their hair and throw themselves on their loved ones' graves. There is an exquisite edge to things: their sorrow is deeper, their joy is sweeter. And, I would add, they are doing exactly what they need to be doing. Depression is a natural stage of mourning—or so we used to think. In the latest edition of the *Diagnostic and Statistical Manual of Mental Disorders* by the American Psychiatric Association (DSM-5), grief is now a categorized mental illness and can be treated accordingly, with medications. Eli Lilly already has an antidepressant, Cymbalta, in clinical trials for "bereavement-related depression."

———

In addition to our beliefs, those who work with the dying also bring what they don't yet know about themselves to the work. We don't know our toleration level or saturation point; we don't know what enough will look like. Susan, who burned out after eighteen years on the job, calculated that she had helped over seven hundred people die. She left hospice and went to work in labour and delivery, where she vowed to deliver seven hundred babies before she retired. We don't know that sometimes we will be profoundly moved by the beauty of a death and other times we will be horrified by the reality.

*WHAT WE BELIEVE DIRECTLY INFLUENCES HOW WE ACT. AMONGST
the Salish, the dead are never far away, and the living have
a responsibility to remember them and look after them
in the spirit world. If they are hungry, they must be fed; if
they are cold, clothes must be sent over to them. Ghosts, left
unattended or ignored, can be harmful to the living. After
a funeral, a burning is often held to cook for the dead and
send over their valued possessions. Kindling and newspapers
are spread on the ground and cedar planks laid overtop. This
"table" is then laid with their favourite foods and set on fire.*

*It is a surreal feeling to cook for the dead. The day I
cooked for my brother, thirty-five years after his death, I felt
like a cross between the Galloping Gourmet and Morticia
Addams. At the time, my community was largely made up
of Salish family and friends, and while I had taken part in a
number of burnings, I had never cooked for a family member.*

*Lena is in her seventies. I first met her at a communal
burning in the Upper Squamish Valley, where, from time to
time, burnings are arranged when it is believed that the spirits
are unsettled—when dogs bark all night long for no reason,
or voices are heard singing the old songs up the river. Her
daughters take turns driving her to town for groceries and
picking her up on the afternoons she plays bingo. Pictures of
her twenty-five grandchildren are tacked up on her living
room walls, and most days you will find her knitting for one
of them with the hand-spun wool she keeps in green garbage
bags in her bedroom closet. Lena is also a shaker: the person
you go to when there is a problem with ghosts. She and others
who belong to the Shaker Church are mediators between the
living and the dead. She knows what the dead are craving. At*

one burning I attended, a family, whose baby had died many years ago, placed a baby bottle on the table. Boiling milk exploded out of the bottle and shot straight up through the flames, and everybody there knew that the baby had waited a long time to drink.

I called my mother to ask her what Ian's favourite food had been. "Crepes," she answered, without hesitation. It was not unusual, she said, for him to eat a dozen with sugar and fresh lemon for breakfast. The ingredients are simple: flour, eggs, milk and a pinch of salt. I started crying and talking to him as soon as I began mixing the batter. Had you happened to look through the kitchen window, you would have thought I was hammered.

The burning took place on a sandy estuary on the Tsawout reserve. It was a warm Sunday in May; the air was heavy with the scent of wild rose, and the nearby hills were dense with red and yellow Scotch broom. Lena had cooked spaghetti and meatballs and lemon meringue pie for her relatives, and when we were done setting up I realized we had a couple of extra servings. Lena told us to put them on the table, as there are always unexpected guests. My mother, who had come over for the day, stood beside me while I placed the crepes on top of the wood and the paper was set on fire.

Fires for the dead seem to burn with a particular intensity. Blue flames curl around the plates of food in slow motion; the flames burn so hot and high that the fire is smokeless. In the Quran, smokeless fire refers to the tips of flames out of which the jinn were created—the genies in Arab folklore that occupy a parallel world to ours. In the fire that day, on the beach, we could see the genie unleashed.

The Mexican poet Octavio Paz observes that Mexicans have no qualms about getting close with death. On Día de Muertos, thousands of candles are lit and placed on altars and graves; if the candles are blown out, the spirits leave. The Mexican, he says, "chases after it, mocks it, courts it, sleeps with it; it is his favourite plaything and most lasting love."

At one point, when the plates were cracking and fire had consumed the whole table, my mother, who was standing beside me, collapsed against my side. "I didn't know," she whispered. "I didn't know."

"What?" I asked, alarmed. "What is it?"

"I didn't know they were together," she said. "I didn't know John was with him."

John, Ian's father, died shortly after the war, when Ian was a young boy. My secular English mother did not have one doubt in her body that the ghosts of her late husband and son had come to the table together that day to eat crepes drizzled with lemon and sugar.

The Pied Piper

I can't say that, as time went on, it got easier to be with the dying. There was an intensity to the work that was seductive: it was both exhausting and full of wonder. For a long time I couldn't imagine doing anything else. Each situation brought new challenges. One night when I was working on the crisis team, we were called to pronounce the death of a Scottish man we had met earlier that day. Susan, the nurse I was with, suggested to the family that we could dress him in his traditional regalia.

It is hard work dressing the dead. I did not find it easy to touch a body the way many of the nurses did. My training was geared to the psychological; there were no smells involved in my training, no body fluids, catheters, suction tubes, no bags of saline or blood to hang on IV poles, no ostomy bags with fecal waste, or fungating tumours to dress.

Susan was compassionate and pragmatic. She started on the unit as a volunteer and decided to leave her dental assistant's job to study nursing when she saw how kind nurses were with the dying. In nursing school, she remembers Sister Ida telling the students, "You can't relieve spiritual suffering until you first relieve physical suffering." Susan took that as her motto. When I asked her about her ease with dead bodies, she mused that maybe it was because nurses are so familiar with naked bodies before death. There is an intimacy that comes from looking after ill people, she believes—"an intimacy that often opens a pathway to tending emotional and spiritual needs." Performing physical care is one of the first things nurses do. "Right after we introduce ourselves," says Susan. Where else, other than brothels, do we remove our clothes before the introductions are complete?

Susan motioned for me to get on the bed after she had removed the catheter and subcutaneous butterflies and lightly washed the body. I sat back to back with the corpse and propped my feet up against the headboard to give myself leverage while she squeezed, tugged, hauled and cinched a thirty-four-inch kilt around a forty-two-inch, ascites-swollen waist. We looked as if we were in a Monty Python skit on the set of *Night of the Living Dead*. She eased his rigid arms into a long-sleeved white shirt with ruffles down the front, pulled on his knee socks, clipped on his garters and cut the back of his jacket in half so that she could button up the front. She fluffed the pillow while I extricated myself, and looped the sporran and chains through the belt loops at the back of the kilt. She laid him out like a fierce Highlander.

It was a warm July night; although it was the height of summer, you could already smell autumn in the air. A few minutes after we arrived, the patient's son left the room shaking and crying; a shy man, he had not spoken to us at all. Almost immediately after we'd finished bathing and dressing the body, we heard a sound outside. At first it seemed like a high cry, a keening, but when we got up and looked out of the window, we realized the son was walking slowly around the outside of the house playing the bagpipes, piping his father out. With each note, porch lights flicked on in the neighbourhood and people came outside. They were drawn from their homes the way the children of Hamelin were drawn to the Pied Piper; they came out to stand in the night air, and had the piper walked down the street and kept going on his way to the distant mountains, they would have followed. I would have, too.

Mercy

At three o'clock one morning, when a nurse was returning to the unit after a busy night, a rabbit darted in front of the car and lay stunned on the road after the impact. The nurse got out of her car, unlocked the trunk, opened the drug kit, drew up fifty milligrams of morphine and euthanized the bunny. Nothing else was going to suffer that night. Not on her shift. No way.

The Dying Never Take Planes

When I was a kid, I often spoke in code with my friends. We lived in what we thought was a secret world: *ets-lay lay-pay owboys-cay and-ay Indians-ay*. It was a world that was perfectly clear to us but not always decipherable to those who didn't understand pig Latin. When we encountered somebody who spoke our language fluently, we experienced it as a kind of instant intimacy—as if they could see what we saw, feel what we felt, as if they had entered our world, were a part of our secret society.

Language, says ethnobotanist Wade Davis, is not simply a set of grammatical rules or vocabulary; it is a flash of the human spirit, a window of sorts into the cosmology of our lives. Nowhere is the power of language more evident than in our language around death. My husband, Patrick, grew up in Steinbach, Manitoba, a small Mennonite town on the prairies. His father died at age fifty-five, leaving behind a young family. When Patrick wrote in the obituary that his father had died, the pastor at his father's church stroked out the word *died* and replaced it with *passed away*. Death was not an end in the town with twenty-six churches and a population of around three thousand; it was a passage to another life. A new beginning.

Rarely is death called by its own name.

Euphemism, meaning "to speak with good words, to use good words of omen," derived from the Greek *eu* "good" and *pheme* "speaking," is most often associated with denial in the West—evidence of our discomfort in speaking directly about death—and yet, at the same time that it helps us to avoid forbidden topics, it also offers a way to voice the unspeakable. Certain experiences are too intimate to be talked about without safeguards. In many cultures, there is a reluctance—based on fear, superstition or taboo—to talk about death directly. We reach for language that will soften the blow. Some Australian tribes are forbidden to say the name of the deceased for one year, during which time they also avoid words that rhyme with the name of the dead person. In a ceremony at the end of the year, when the name of the deceased is spoken, it is a way to welcome him or her back into the lives of the living. Salish people will not talk about funeral arrangements while someone is dying, as to do so invites death into the house. Pablo Picasso refused to make a will as a way of avoiding death—leaving his family to fight over a $30-million estate. His son Paolo was quoted as saying, "The death of my father raises grave problems for the family."

Many of the euphemisms we use about death are based on the Christian hope of resurrection. People are said to *pass away* or *depart*, as if they are embarking on a journey; we are told they are *resting in peace* or *in a better place* or that they *have gone home to be with their maker*. "We are *in* this world," Patrick was told, "but not *of* this world." At its best, euphemism allows us to skirt around the taboos surrounding human mortality; at its worst, it is a sentimental Hallmark response to suffering.

———

Whereas euphemism averts its gaze in relation to death, metaphor speaks to the mystery at the heart of it. Metaphor, the engine of poetry, is also the language of the dying. Many people, in their last days, speak of one thing in terms of another. Medical language is primarily utilitarian; it does not depend on rhetorical, metaphorical or other poetic effects.

I have atrial tachycardia. When my heart bursts out of the starting gate, I don't want my doctor commenting on the race; I want him to calculate the amount of propofol needed to put me under and how many joules of electricity it will take to shock my heart back to sinus rhythm.

The origins of medical terminology, however, are highly metaphoric. According to the human anatomy textbook *Gray's Anatomy*, *coccyx*, the Greek word for "cuckoo," refers to the bird's beak and its likeness to our tailbone; *atrium*, the word for "hall" or "entrance," is used for the upper chamber of the heart; *glans* comes from the Latin for "acorn" and is used for the head of the penis, which is somewhat shaped like an acorn. *Morphine* is derived from Morpheus, Ovid's name for the god of dreams.

Beneath the terminology is a world rich in mythology, a world that Niels Bohr, the father of quantum physics, believed was so complex that to describe it fully one must use the language of poetry. The role of metaphor, Bohr proposed, was essential even in scientific thought. There are numerous reasons, including drug reactions and disease process, why somebody who is dying might be incoherent, but there are instances in which we don't hear what they are saying because we haven't learned to listen: we haven't entered their world.

Pain speaks a number of languages. On one level it needs no translation; on another level it requires that we become translators and interpreters if we are to be of any help. The doctors and nurses who do this work understand the language of pain. They have as many words for pain as one imagines the Bedouin must have for wind (the Inuit, we are now told, really have only twelve words for snow): *sharp, dull, aching, crushing, searing, tingling, red, white, hot, cold, malevolent, familiar, catlike, ghostlike, jabbing, nagging, scalding, flickering, ravenous, blinding, shooting, boring, wrenching, nauseating.*

In her essay "On Being Ill," Virginia Woolf wrote, "English, which can express the thoughts of Hamlet and the tragedy of Lear, has no words for the shiver and the headache. . . . Let the sufferer try to describe a pain in his head to a doctor and language at once runs dry." For some, it just hurts like hell; for others, there are no words at all.

Those who encounter the dying must learn to think like the poet who reaches for language the way a child reaches for the moon, believing it can be held in the hand like an orange at the same time as it shines on in the night sky.

Without metaphor, how could we understand the man, dying of leukemia, with four sons, who tells his youngest, "The road was never marked very clearly, I kept missing the turns, now the vehicle is out of gas." Or the woman who asks, "Where will I live when they jackhammer my street?" How could we see what the woman crouched on her knees on her hospital bed sees when she smiles and tells the doctor she is peeking into heaven? How could we comprehend the Buddhist woman who, in the hours before her death, insists that the heads of all the flowers in her garden be chopped off in case the smell of jasmine, rose, lavender and lilac hold her back? Without metaphor, how could we comprehend, as Robert Desnos did, that the earth is a camp lit by thousands of spiritual fires whose sparks rise and burn through the roof of the tent?

When his grandfather, Herman, was in a coma, my son-in-law, Lee, slept beside him on a cot in the Rose Room—a room reserved for the dying—at the local hospital. Waiting is often hard. Earlier in the day, Herman had said, "I am ready, but which door do I take?" Before going to sleep, Lee covered his grandfather with a hand-spun Native blanket. In the night, a nurse drew back the blanket because he was hot. Shortly after this, he died. The blanket, given to him by his grandson, was the door.

"Every metaphor," writes Jane Hirshfield, "every hymn-shout of praise, points to the shared existence of beings and things."

———————

The language of the dying is not static; it is a language of movement, of platforms, tickets, passports and maps, visitations and greetings, entrances and exits. A language of arrivals and departures. They will often ask if their bags are packed or if there is a full tank of gas in the car. They repeat themselves, asking if the train is on time; asking if you will be coming with them. You must enter this as you would enter a foreign land; signs will be of little help. You must see what they see. It is never planes they wait for; rather, they pull away slowly from this earth—the fields of fall rye rolling as far as the eye can see.

It is an esemplastic language that sees this world at the same time as it sees another. Much like the White Rabbit in *Alice in Wonderland*, the dying too are often preoccupied with time. *I'm late, I'm late for a very important date; no time to say hello, goodbye, I'm late, I'm late, I'm late.* Sometimes they wait for someone to arrive from out of town; sometimes they die when people have stepped out of the room for five minutes to have a smoke. One day in ICU a boy who had been hanging on for weeks, after an accident, died within minutes of his mother telling him it was okay to go. The wonder is not that the dying might wait—that a boy might need his mother's permission—but that the living might sometimes be able to open the door for them.

One man told me he was going hiking in the mountains but was a bit anxious because he didn't have a map. Another man, on his deathbed, told his wife a yellow cab had pulled up in front of their house.

"The fool's got the wrong address," he said, "but since he's here, I may as well go."

His wife looked out the window to the empty street and said, "Yes, love, you might as well."

The metaphors of departure and everlasting life do not apply as readily to sudden death. There is an uncertainty to the language, a flicker of doubt. Where was God, we wonder, when *life was cut short* and someone *was taken from us*? Where was He the night my brother was killed? When something is killed, life is, by definition, extinguished. That feels accurate. Ian was snuffed out like a candle. One minute there was light; the next we were standing, disoriented, trying to adjust our eyes to the pervasive dark.

In the introduction to the 2011 edition of *Best American Essays*, Edwidge Danticat writes, "Through recent experiences with both birth and death, I have discovered that we enter and leave life as, among other things, words." Many of us start life, she muses, as whispers or rumours. Born into language, we take in the sound of voices, the sound of wind in the trees, the clattering of dishes, the cooing voices of our mothers, the day-to-day prattle that goes on above our cribs, and we make, of this, our native tongue. On our way out, we may once again speak the indecipherable language of our childhood kingdoms.

Sometimes there are no explanations for the languages we speak. Years ago, Thais, a cousin by marriage, told me that her youngest child's first words were in the old Squamish dialect. The baby was raised, as most Salish babies are now, in an English-speaking home. Last year, my friend Delmar Johnnie, or Seletze as he was known by his ancestral name, died of complications due to multi-system atrophy. In his obituary, our mutual friend Chris Welsh wrote, "Delmar often told of how, as a young boy, he loved to fish in the Cowichan River near his home at Green Point, B.C. He sometimes watched an old man across the water cleaning fish and singing as he worked. One day he sang the song he'd heard the old man singing and his grandmother asked him where he'd heard it. The song belonged to his great-grandfather, Seletze, who was in the spirit world."

———————

Some metaphorical thinking—such as that described by Susan Sontag in *Illness as Metaphor*—may be counterproductive. When someone with cancer is told their "anger" contributed to the disease or there is a suggestion that a person gets an illness because "they have something to learn," it is both untrue and unhelpful. At a symbolic and metaphoric level, death is used to understand other realities in human life. In Chinese tradition, if a woman's fiancé died before the wedding, she could choose to go through with the ceremony, in which a white cockerel would represent the groom. This "ghost marriage" ensured that the woman still had access to a male descent line and would be cared for after her death. The wife of a ghost was required to take a vow of celibacy and immediately take up residence with his family. In this way she became part of the family and legitimacy was maintained. Sometimes it was arranged for two ghosts to marry if the family got wind that one or the other was lonely.

"Illness," wrote Sontag, "is the night side of life. Everyone who is born holds dual citizenship, in the kingdom of the well and in the kingdom of the sick." The use of metaphor, in both these kingdoms, makes room for the imagination. It allows the mind to walk towards death without having to confront it directly. It allows ghosts to marry.

———————

The body speaks a number of languages. On one level, it needs no translation; on another, it requires that we become translators and interpreters if we are to be of any help. Whenever I'm away on a trip, I know that I will start to return home in my imagination at least two days before actually leaving. The dying too will often withdraw from loved ones days before death; they often leave us before we let go of them. Over the years it became apparent to me that the dying regularly shove off from shore before untying the bowline. Some kick off blankets and remove their clothing, as if fighting their way back to the womb. Some turn to face the wall and disappear into an opening only they can see. It wasn't until I read Jane Kenyon's poem "Reading Aloud to My Father" that I understood the living, too, must play their part and resist the urge to haul the skiff back in:

> *At the end they don't want their hands*
> *to be under the covers, and if you should put*

your hand on theirs in a tentative gesture
of solidarity, they'll pull their hand free;
and you must honour that desire,
and let them pull it free.

When family members struggled with a perceived rejection, it was sometimes helpful to suggest that their loved one was not turned away from them as much as turned towards something else. It was necessary to learn to read the body; to differentiate between physical pain and other kinds of suffering. To know when to intervene and when to stand back and let the dying sort through whatever it was they were working out.

If it is close to impossible to translate the music at the heart of poetry, then the same must be said for any attempts to precisely translate the dying process. The word *translation* derives from the Latin *translatus*, meaning "to bring over, carry over." To *translate* is "to remove from one place to another."

Seen in this light, death itself is an act of translation.

"Poetry's fertility," writes Jane Hirshfield, "lives in the marriage of the said and the unsaid, of languaged self and unlanguaged other, of the knowable world and the gravitational pull of what lies beyond knowing." We can interpret the physical signs of dying, but there remains an element of the untranslatable in both poetry and dying. A mystery at the heart of both. Something only the dying know.

The elegiac nature of poetry is derived from human grief. If poetry is how we speak to the dead, and if metaphor is the language that waits for us at the end, it is poets who help us understand death, because they are using that language now. The poet listens to water, to the wind, to the back alleys of sweltering cities; she sees the old fence falling down and hears the first nail that was driven into it; she attempts to sit with what is and not what she assumes something to be. The poet makes great leaps from the known world into the unknown, from the rational to the irrational, the steady to the unsteady. The dying, too, make great leaps from the known to the unknown, from the rational to the symbolic.

I inherited a dark forest, but today I am walking in the other forest, the light one. We are, all of us, walking along with the poet Tomas Tranströmer in a forest of light. It will not always be so.

In the days and hours before an expected death, many people enter a kind of altered state. It is clear, when you look at them, that they are looking through you to something else. A story is told about the time W. H. Auden, walking across the grounds at Oxford, immersed in a discussion about poetry with a group of students, had to be guided by one of them around a gaping hole in the ground. Teased about this, Auden is reported to have said, "I am not absent-minded, I am present-minded elsewhere."

The Talmud teaches that unborn children are in a holy state. They are visited, in the womb, by the angels of light and sadness and taught the Torah and the secrets of creation. Just before they are born, Purah, the angel of forgetfulness, taps them over the lips and they forget everything, but an echo stays *in the deep stronghold of the heart*. If birth is a kind of forgetting, could dying be a kind of remembering? Are the dying present-minded elsewhere?

When we leave, is there a stream of light that continues for a while after we're gone? When we observe the crab nebula, for example, we are seeing it not as it is now, but how it was four thousand years ago. In the elapsing of one minute, a star ten thousand light years away from earth explodes and it ceases to exist. Five thousand years after this explosion, we still see the light. You get the idea. Of course, there's always Wikipedia to help with these things: "Imagine I dropped a letter in the snail mail then dropped dead. It's like asking how long my letter could go on after I died. The answer is 'until it is delivered.' My death doesn't stop the letter from coming."

The metaphoric language of the dying is the language of the boatman. Of the five rivers dividing Hades, it is Acheron, the river of sorrow, across which Charon ferries the newly dead. It is the river Lethe they drink from to forget their past lives. The difference between *translation* and *metaphor* is slight—the former meaning "to bring or carry over"; the latter, derived from the Greek, "to transfer or carry across." If death is an act of translation, metaphor, then, is the language of transition. You could say it is the falsework, the scaffolding of the whole dying process; it holds us up until the crossing is strong enough to get us to the other side.

In Athens, three-wheeled delivery trucks, used to transport merchandise around the city, career through the streets with *Metaphor* written on their sides, causing pedestrians to jump out of the way and curse them with their own metaphors.

Aristotle believed the use of metaphor was a sign of genius. The dying as geniuses. On some level we know we will all be there one day. Climbing into the yellow cab idling at the front door.

From the Dictionary of Angels

Angelos, from the Greek, means "messenger," either human or divine. In rabbinical teachings there are at least a dozen angels of death—Adriel, Apollyon-Abaddon, Leviathan, Malach ha-Mavet, Metatron and Yehudiah, to name a few. With those monikers, there's no mistaking them for Gentiles. In Christian tradition, the angel Gabriel is the angel of consolation. Michael, the angel of death, "leads souls into the eternal light" at the yielding up of the ghost of all good Christians. Michael is made up entirely of snow, Gabriel of fire. "And though they stand near one another they do not injure one another." So says the Rabbi Akiva. I would have thought the angel of death was made of fire, but no, God has His own ideas about consolation. Fire, it seems, figures prominently in His plans; the seraphs are born of a stream of it blazing out from under His throne.

In Muslim theology, Azrael is the angel of death who is forever writing in a large book and forever erasing what he writes. What he writes is the birth of man, what he erases is the name of the man at death. One wonders at the futility of this; one wonders if there are times he just wants to skip over a few names, put his feet up, call it a day.

Josef Mengele, the infamous Nazi doctor, nicknamed the Angel of Death for his diabolical experiments on twins in Auschwitz, was also known as the White Angel for the calculating, cold manner in which he chose who would live and who would die when the trains pulled into the camp each day. Angel Dust showed up on the streets of San Francisco in the 1960s—otherwise known as PCP, Peace Pill, crystal, hog, horse tranquilizer, embalming fluid and rocket fuel. People were known to take flying leaps out of windows, like angels, when high on the stuff.

What's in a name? Joe Fortes arrived in Vancouver from Barbados in 1883. He worked as a shoeshine boy and porter in the city where, seventy years later, I was born. Joe pitched a tent on English Bay and took to patrolling the beach as a self-appointed lifeguard; legend has it that hundreds were saved on his watch. In 1901, the city appointed him its first official lifeguard. Joe's full name was Seraphim "Joe" Fortes. Named by his mother after the highest order of angels, Joe, it seems, just had an instinct for the drowning.

———

When I was sixteen, on my way back home from a track meet, I was thrown seventy feet when the car I was riding in was struck by a semi running a red light. What a passerby would have seen was a girl hurtling through the air—a human projectile. What I remember is the silence, reading the letters on the side of the truck, falling in slow motion through space. I came to, on the ground, in the arms of a stranger. It felt as if I was cushioned. Laid down so gently, caught by what, or whom, I can't really say.

I like to think my brother experienced something close to this. Something other than what Bowering described in his poem as a *horrid air-filled explosion, shrieking steel . . . a twirling upside down rubber wheel, sirens*. But I don't know. The writer Christopher Dewdney, who was a passenger in a streetcar that was blindsided by another streetcar one late spring afternoon, remembers people flying out of their seats and safety glass erupting like a floating mist all around him; but mostly he remembers that all of it took place in deafening silence, in slow motion. "It seems," he writes, that "we are able to experience accelerated time for brief periods. But we cannot experience anything like what high-speed film can capture now—bullets slowly plunging through apples, hovering hummingbirds flapping their wings at the speed of a crow." For a brief moment we are outside time. Falling through the air. Caught by what or whom we cannot say.

Time changes for the dying too. In the last days and hours, they often seem preoccupied and outside time as we know it. Joseph lived most of his life on boats that he built and sailed around the world. He was always working: sewing sails, fixing rigging, sanding and varnishing the decks. There was an oak tree outside his hospice room. When I visited him shortly before his death, he told me, "One leaf falling can occupy me all day."

Angels were often left by patients' families in a small alcove in the hospice unit: some with their heads bowed in prayer, some looking skyward; crystal angels from Birks and plastic angels from Walmart; winged and haloed last hopes, with the tacky, overly religious and just plain ugly ones being culled from time to time. For those who wanted inspiration, there was a shell with angel cards beside a white porcelain angel with a worried look on her face.

Far from the fiery six-winged beings crying "Holy, holy, holy!" with their flaming swords held high, angels today have come to represent sentimental presences that shine with New Age light and can be purchased everywhere from hospital gift shops to the china section in thrift stores where the glass ashtrays used to be. People often called us angels when we arrived on their doorsteps, but it was our strangeness with death as much as our familiarity with it that allowed us to help in whatever ways we could. Angels we were not.

"Estrangement is at the root of suffering," writes Rabbi Dayle Friedman in *Jewish Pastoral Care.* Caregivers must find the stranger in themselves to understand what it might be like for the dying who are becoming estranged from all that is known.

According to Miriam, who calls upon her Jewish faith in the work she does, there is a notion that Jews should be kind to strangers because they too were strangers in a strange land. "I was excited by the connection to strangers," she told me, "because it disrupted the favoured metaphors of angels and 'special people' doing 'special work.'" The truth of it, she says, is that this work is best done by people who have hovered on the outside edges of comfort, by choice or circumstance or temperament. People, a little rough around the edges, who have seen a few things. In a society that encourages us to shy away from death, we had to learn how to walk towards it. To open the door and make ourselves at home.

Miriam recently wrote to me,

> Last Friday, I went into a patient's room. I had heard, during the morning report from her nurse, that this woman was terrified. She had been distressed all night, struggling and frightened. Many drugs were given. I went in to offer presence to the patient and her two daughters. I had never met any of them before that morning. When I entered the room the patient was unconscious; her daughters were teary, but calm, aware that death was near, hoping that death was near. I hung out, asked questions, sat on the pull-out bed with one of the daughters. I heard about how their mom had already told them that she wanted egg salad sandwiches at her funeral.
>
> They mentioned going to Catholic school as girls. I asked them if their mom was still connected to the Church and if she might want prayers? They paused and looked at one another, paused for a bit longer and finally they said, "Well, really, she identified more with Judaism in recent years; her paternal grandmother was Jewish. . . . She went to

the synagogue downtown but we don't know much about that."

I asked if I could sing the Shema *for their mom—the* Shema *is traditionally sung by the dying person or by someone who cares for them. They said yes. I went and stood by her head, the dying woman, and I took her hand and told her my name. She did not respond; however, as soon as I sang the first word, she gasped and opened her eyes and her energy fluttered. I sang, Shema Yisrael, adonei, elo-heinu, adonei ehad two or three times. Her breathing settled. I paused and told them a little more and sang a few more times. Her breathing slowed. She died.*

The whole thing, from the first sung word to her last breath, might have lasted two minutes. No more.

The wonder is not that Miriam knew what to do and did it well; rather, the wonder is in the randomness of it all. Not the "sacredness" of the story, which so easily dips into the precious. The wonder is that she walked into that room at that time without any notion of what might be helpful, and was used in the service of the good. That's the thing. To be used in the service of the good.

———————

My favourite angels are the pen-and-ink ones sketched by the painter and poet Joe Rosenblatt: angels with fur, cat angels, sunny angels being carried off by a flock of bright blue birds.

The preternatural critters—downy angels and demons—that materialized in the bat cave of his imagination.

"Now a demon or daemon can be bipolar, benevolent or downright malevolent, depending on cultural environment," says Joe. "Angels generally are not seen in a bad light. I certainly try to give demons parity in my drawings, although my bias favours the angels. The demons are generally benign in my visual window, and yet my cat angel or angels in fur have fearsome expressions, as though they have just lunched on the proverbial mine songbird."

Animals

What, I wonder, do animals know about death? The red horses of Irish mythology are death horses; in the Book of Revelation, Death himself arrives on a pale horse. In Egyptian funerary relics, the spine of a snake was said to contain the fluid of death; on the other hand, the spine of a bull, considered the source of semen, was the fluid of life. Birds, by the very fact that they are not earthbound, are often seen as portentous. Swallows, in ancient mythology, bore the displeasure of the gods; in England, a swallow trapped in the house was believed to be a sign of death; purple martins, on the other hand, were viewed as serving God and were known as his "bow and arrow." The idea of hundreds of them plucked from God's quiver and fired to earth—with their slightly forked tails and tucked wings—goes a long way in tempering the idea of a wrathful celestial archer.

The Egyptians believed the souls of the dead took the form of bees and ascended alive into heaven; with an unerring sense of the soul, lost far from Amenta's fields, they made a beeline for home. I met a woman once who made a beeline after weeks in a coma seemingly unable to die. The woman's hospital bed was in her living room looking out on the ponds and pathways she had spent years creating. The nurse and I arrived, as we had every morning, to draw up meds and visit with her daughter. On this particular day, a bee buzzed incessantly against the inside of the sliding glass door directly in front of the patient's bed. Without thinking, I walked over and slid the door open. In the time it took the bee to crawl over the metal rim and fly out towards the garden, the woman took two breaths and was gone.

It's easy, in the presence of death, to see the extraordinary in the ordinary; harder to know what is imagined, or hoped for, and what is real. On the morning of my mother's funeral, hundreds of honey bees filled the chapel—released overnight from the numerous flowers that had been delivered. At her service, their steady hum rose and fell like the undisciplined chorus of an audience before a concert; the room vibrated with anticipation and out of the corner of our eyes the bees, moving in and out of the long shafts of light, tricked us into thinking the air was flecked with moving gold. That same morning, my son, who had returned from Ghana for his Nani's funeral, awoke to find an *Apis mellifera scutellata*, otherwise known as an African killer bee, on his pillow. For three days we saw bees everywhere.

To find a honey tree, says Annie Dillard, catch a bee when its legs are heavy with pollen and it is ready for home. Release it and follow it for as long as you can see it; wait until another bee comes, catch it, release and follow it. Keep doing this and sure enough it will lead you home. Sometimes all we can do is catch the impulses that feel right to us and follow them until we lose them. Who knows, if there is a spirit, how it leaves? We don't know, but every window on the hospice unit is open just a crack—just in case. Bee to bee leading us home.

In early traditions, bees were believed to have originated in paradise and were known as "little servants of the gods." At my mother's funeral, the little servants flew above our heads like scullery maids in the great house.

One of the hallmarks of grief is our need to make sense of loss. It is not uncommon to look for a sign, a message more or less signalling, "I'm gone but I'm still here." Animal sightings are sometimes *interpreted* as visitations. A few days after my friend's mother died, a hummingbird hovered outside her kitchen window while she was washing dishes. A sign is a combination of things—a confluence of our hopes, memories, beliefs—a moment in which the veil seems to drop and we are granted a glimpse of another reality.

For my friend, the fact that it was winter and hummingbirds were her mother's favourite birds was enough for her to believe that her mother had come to say goodbye. The word *interpretation* lends a certain kind of bias to the idea of signs. I don't know if her mother did pay her a visit, but I also don't know that she didn't. Ten years after his father died, Patrick awoke to see a disc of fire spinning in his room like a buzz saw blade. At first he thought it was God, but quickly understood it was his father saying goodbye. Now, he says, perhaps there is no difference between the two.

For the hunter, a set of prints in the snow reveal the deer that is nowhere in sight. We seek the invisible through the visible. We discern God, as the sixteenth-century Anabaptist leader Pilgram Marpeck wrote, through the beauty of his works.

"If you had told me twenty years ago that the children in our Texas towns would have green hair and bones in their noses," says the sheriff of El Paso to Tommy Lee Jones in the film *No Country for Old Men*, "I just flat out wouldn't have believed it."

"Signs and wonders," sighs Jones. "Signs and wonders."

———————

What do animals know? Do they sense our sadness or do they have their own? My father left when I was five. Soon after, our dachshund, Lucy, died. My mother told me she had died of a broken heart. We see the heart in our mind's eye. I used to imagine Lucy's made of red construction paper torn down the middle. Other times, I saw it explode in her chest in a bloody pulp.

There are dogs that smell drugs, cancer, bombs, diabetes, blood, gasoline and bedbugs. Specially trained cadaver dogs sniff out human remains; guide dogs act as our eyes and ears. Scientists are working on an early warning detection system using dogs that sniff out various illnesses in the hope of staving off death by refining early diagnoses and treatment. A boy in Timmins, Ontario, has a diabetes dog that can dial 911. We fight death with everything in our arsenal; when machines fail us, we call out the pack. We are relentless, but perhaps not quite as relentless as our furred friends who would do anything for us—including risk their own lives—for a treat and the chance to chase after the small orange ball we keep tucked away in our back pockets.

In Hindu mythology, dogs are believed to be messengers of Yama, the god of death, and are said to whine and whimper when they sense death approaching. I've never seen a dog act this way. In the houses I attended, most dogs just seemed sad. In one home, I confused the patient's name with his dog's name and sternly ordered the patient "down" when the dog jumped on me. In another, a border collie herded me away from the door every time I tried to leave. Very few barked; mostly, they were curled up on their owners' beds, where they stayed, often refusing to eat, until the person died.

There is a difference between seeing and wanting to see something; between a genuine encounter and wishful thinking. After my mother's death, I went looking for a sign. I drove three hundred miles to the northernmost tip of Vancouver Island with my two daughters. I didn't know where we were going, I just wanted to drive until the road ended and we could go no farther. We stopped for candy at the Sayward general store and bought wool and needles in Port McNeill, where we stayed overnight in a cheap motel and I tried to teach my daughters to knit just as my mother had taught me in 1969. Hopeless, they abandoned their knitting efforts after half an hour, and we ended up lying on the bed watching the one working channel on the TV. We fell asleep fully clothed and in the morning we headed to Cape Scott and hiked the trail to San Josef Bay through old-growth forest and emerged onto a white sand beach on which stunted cedars, like bonsai, grew on top of hollowed-out stacks of volcanic rock. It was breathtakingly beautiful, but it wasn't beauty I was seeking. I wanted a sign.

After she died, I thought to myself that if only it could get silent enough, I might be able to hear her. If people stopped talking; if the wind died down; if the noise of traffic, the hum of wires, the sound of birds flying, cellphones, radios, the washer on spin cycle, someone clearing their throat—if only the sound of my own thoughts would die down, then maybe I would hear her and know where she had disappeared to.

We fanned out on the beach, connected but separate like a splayed hand. I scanned the sky for eagles and walked along the creek looking for otters—her favourite animal. Bears and cougars had been sighted in recent days, but I saw nothing, not even tracks. Two crows nattered at each other, but she hated crows and would have been offended if I took their appearance as a sign. She was gone. There was nowhere on earth I would find her. There were no messages, no sightings, no possible interpretations of a spiritual existence. No spinning discs; only the relentless pounding of the surf and a cold March wind kicking up a few sand spouts along the empty beach. It was the magnitude of the nothing that took my breath away.

Many First Nations people on the coast believe the owl represents death. My ex-husband, a hereditary chief, believed the owl travelled between the land of the living and the land of the dead. One day, when he was driving down a logging road on his way back from hunting, a barred owl landed in front of his truck. His uncle, in the passenger seat, started shaking, and upon arriving home he was told that a close relative had died. If an owl lands in front of my truck and I don't share the cultural belief, what then? After my marriage ended, it took me a long time to see the owl as simply a bird and not some messenger of death.

Years ago, I was given two tabby cats by a friend on the local reserve. The cats, a brother and sister, fit perfectly in the palms of my hands. The female, Tigger, was short-haired and petite, fine-boned and delicate like Audrey Hepburn. Her brother, Askem, long-haired and scrappy, was more like Keith Richards. In sleep, curled up together, you couldn't tell one from the other. When Askem died after being hit by a car in front of the house, we sprinkled dried flowers over his body and buried him in a shoebox in the back garden. Whenever Tigger went outside, she made her way directly to the grave and curled up on it until we brought her in at night. It's easy to anthropomorphize animals—to imagine Tigger grieving for her brother. I don't know why she slept on his grave every day for a year and then abruptly changed to a sunny spot in the woodpile. Maybe she missed him, or smelled him, or maybe it was simply the warmest spot in the garden. Maybe her heart was broken. I just don't know.

In her book *A Natural History of the Senses*, Diane Ackerman writes about how animals communicate outside the five senses. Bats and dolphins use ultrasonic or high-pitched sounds, beyond the range of our hearing; elephants and alligators use infrasonic sounds, too low for us to catch. Wind, fire, thunder, floods and earthquakes all emit sounds inaudible to human ears. The language of destruction flies around our heads as we carry on, oblivious. Animals often act in strange ways before an earthquake strikes. There have been reports of catfish leaping out of the water, goats running in circles, dogs howling and elephants screaming. Snakes have been known to leave their underground places of hibernation in the middle of the winter prior to quakes, only to be found frozen on the surface of the snow.

Over the years, I saw numerous animals act in strange, uncharacteristic ways around impending death. In the home of a man dying of lymphoma, a strange cat appeared one day at the far edge of the garden. Nobody recognized it. Every day it came a little closer. The first day it lay on the lawn; the second, it sat on the back porch; the third, it rubbed against the screen door to be let into the sunroom; on the fourth, fifth and sixth days it curled up in a chair at the foot of the patient's bed. From there it climbed onto the bed and made its way slowly up into the man's arms, where it nestled until he died. The man's daughter believed the cat had come to comfort her father. When it disappeared after he died, she put up posters and went door to door trying to find the cat's owner. Nobody recognized it; it was as if it had never existed.

Who knows what an animal knows? According to the *New England Journal of Medicine*, Oscar, the resident cat in a geriatric hospital in Rhode Island, is drawn to the rooms of dying patients and has "presided" over the deaths of twenty-five residents. Completely uninterested in the chronically ill, he scratches to be let in at the doors of imminently dying patients and stays with them until they die. When the undertakers appear, Oscar, who has remained with the body, walks down the corridor with them to the locked door and looks out the window while the hearse drives away.

In ancient Japan, it was thought that somewhere on the tail of a cat there was a single hair that would restore a dying person.

MY BROTHER CHRISTENED MY FIRST DOG WITH CHAMPAGNE. WE'D had dogs before, as a family, but this one was to be mine. The pet, a present from my sister when I was five, was smuggled into the house on Christmas Eve while I was asleep. The dog went out a few times in the night but came back right away — until the last time, when she was let out near dawn.

It's hard to separate memory from imagination. Truth from lies. It was 1958, the year Elvis was inducted into the army and General Charles de Gaulle became prime minister of France; the year Truman Capote wrote Breakfast at Tiffany's *and, according to my mother, the year my father left. He was building a boat in the basement and when it was finished he sailed away. At least that was her story.*

I woke up at seven o'clock and walked sleepily out of my bedroom towards the living room, where I heard my sister crying and my mother consoling her. At the same time, there was a scratch on the door and my brother leapt up and escorted the dog in with a wide sweep of his arm, announcing, in a triumphant voice, as he poured the sparkling wine over her head, "I name you Ruthless!"

There is a larger-than-life quality to big brothers. A mythology. They are the ones who can do no wrong, who are invincible. They are faster than we are, can climb trees in a flash, they tease us and mock us and carry us high on their shoulders, and they belong to no one. They are hungry for everything. Before he left, my father, believing that Ian was on the road to becoming a juvenile delinquent, got him a job at one of the radar stations on the DEW Line. When he came home, he brought my mother steak knives with antler handles and a white fox stole that she wore loosely draped over her shoulders.

"*He burned like a wick,*" *wrote his friend George Bowering.* Eyes glazed in utter joy & defiant empty bottle a scepter in his drunken white kingly hand.

In my imagination, when he wasn't with me, my brother lived in a house built of snow and ice and walked on a frozen sea.

El Duende

It was not unusual, when I worked with a nurse on the palliative response crisis team, to be called to see a patient at home in the middle of the night. We would spot the house a block away by the light glowing from one of the bedrooms; most often there was an OXYGEN sign on the door with a red line through it to indicate "no smoking." *Blood of the lamb*, only this time signifying the house had not been passed over. Because we arrived at a time of crisis, all formalities dropped away; we were, in those hours, the closest people on earth to the family. Time slowed, the way it does in a crisis, the neighbourhood slept on. Death was a presence that shared the night with us; not the Grim Reaper or the black angel, not the rider on his pale horse or Allah's Azrael. It was something quieter than that. It was in the rocking branches and in the voice serenading; it entered us from the soles of our feet.

In some strange way we needed death's presence on our visits to the dying. There are no words in English to explain this; the closest, in Spanish, is *el duende*. "There are," wrote Lorca, "neither maps nor exercises to help us find the *duende*." It is the closest we come to raw emotion—the difference between the trained singer and the one who sings with a scorched throat. "The *duende* loves the rim of the wound," wrote the poet. It is, he said, "a power, not a work. A struggle, not a thought." To be with the dying is not a question of ability or training; it is a work made up of "dark notes."

We visited homes all over the city. People were dying in apartments with intricate intercom systems we had to buzz to gain access to and in leaking condos covered with massive sheets of blue tarp that quivered like sails and filled with wind as if the whole building were setting out to sea. In a one-bedroom apartment on Dallas Road, overlooking the ocean, we met a Japanese woman who told us that souls come in with the high tide and leave on the low tide. The greatest high and low tides are the spring tides, when the earth, moon and sun are in line. The moon tries to pull at anything on earth to bring it closer. The earth holds on to everything but water and the rising souls. The woman we met was dying in the fall; she would not be going out on the great low tide, she would have to settle instead for the neap tide at the third quarter of the moon.

We drove our silver palliative-team car down dark streets in sleeping neighbourhoods looking for a certain address; sometimes we'd haul out the spotlight we kept in the back seat and shine it on the houses we drove slowly past like the secret police must have done in some of the villages some of these people came from. We never knew what a shift would bring. One night a doctor called us and asked if we could see a man, with limited English, who was in pain. When we called the home, identifying ourselves as the PRT team, the voice on the other end yelled, "No pizza," and slammed down the phone. Puzzled, we tried calling three times, with the same result, before deciding to just head out. A block away from the house we passed the PT Pizza House and had to stop the car to compose ourselves before knocking on the door.

On Bear Mountain, we met a man, whose wife was dying of Alzheimer's, in a cabin he had built sixty years before.

When she went out for a walk, ten years before we met them, and couldn't find her way home, he built a fence and put in a gate with a lock and lived with her as the world disappeared one word at a time. The name of the mountain disappeared, followed by the name of the nearby town; the way back home was gone around the same time she lost every name for the plants in her garden; she forgot who she was before she forgot who he was. When she began to wander through the rooms at night, and the danger of her burning the place down was real, he put a child's gate up in their bedroom doorway and tucked her into bed. We arrived when she was taking her last breaths; her hair was freshly washed and she was lying under a floral quilt in a clean cotton nightgown. There wasn't much for us to do other than sit with him, after she died, in the small kitchen he had built for her, overlooking the mountain named after a great lumbering beast.

Each shift was different; I never knew, when I showed up for work, where we would go that day. We climbed down ladders into the galleys of sailboats and hiked into the bush to meet people in aluminum trailers. In the home of a compulsive hoarder, we had to walk sideways through stacks of newspapers, old bills, yogurt containers, tins, egg cartons and magazines that formed a kind of maze from the kitchen to the bathroom. The icy blue eyes of hundreds of porcelain dolls, some with flowing curls made out of human hair, followed our every move. When we called the ambulance to take the patient to hospice, they couldn't get the stretcher past the front door. It took two hours to clear a path to get her out.

Years ago, when I read Jane Kenyon's poem "What Came

Me," the image of a hardened drop of gravy on a porcelain gravy boat stayed with me:

> *I took the last*
> *dusty piece of china*
> *out of the barrel.*
> *It was your gravy boat,*
> *with a hard, brown*
> *drop of gravy still*
> *on the porcelain lip.*
> *I grieved for you then*
> *as I never had before.*

We went into homes with china cabinets full of Royal Albert bone china plates, soup tureens and teacups with old country roses on the edges and cut crystal wineglasses that had been handed down for generations. In every one of those cabinets I scanned the shelves looking for a white porcelain gravy boat with a drop of hard brown gravy on the lip. In a house where death had taken up residence, I wanted to see evidence of a life lived. On the kitchen table that was covered with our syringes and vials of morphine, Dilaudid, Haldol, Stemetil, dexamethasone and atropine, I wanted to see wine sloshing in those heavy lead crystal glasses.

Above a Chinese grocery store we met an old man dying of lung cancer in a smoky room with yellowed walls. On the walls were four scrolls with the works of the seventh- and eighth-century poets Li Po, Wang Wei, Jia Dao and Tu Fu. The old man recited, *Drunk, I rise and approach the moon in the stream, birds are far off, people too few.* I wrote the lines down on a piece of scrap paper and stuffed them in my pocket. In that moment it was the poet standing in front of us, not the dying man. I turned to go, completely forgetting that we had come to help because he was short of breath and that his days were very few.

In homes where people could no longer eat, there were cans of strawberry and vanilla Boost on the counter, bowls of ice chips beside the bed and a nearby basin to throw up in. We arrived when things were going wrong—from the Dutch *wrang*, meaning "sour, bitter," literally "that which distorts the mouth." Of all the calls we received, hemorrhages distressed me the most. We were sometimes called to the home of someone who was bleeding out, or "exsanguinating," from the Latin *ex* "out of" and *sanguis* "blood." I dreaded these calls. In one home a dog was licking the blood out of a bucket in front of his owner who was slumped over dead on the couch while *Days of Our Lives* played out on the TV. When she was cleaning the bucket, the nurse beckoned me over to tell me that she had found a lung that he had thrown up. I don't know where to draw the line: what to tell, what not to. Secrecy still surrounds the ways in which we die. There is only so much people want to know. Only so much I can say.

When getting out of bed was no longer an option, we brought commodes and put in catheters. We carried boxes of Depends in the trunk of our car along with six fishing-tackle boxes full of narcotics, stool softeners, sedatives, antipsychotics, antihistamines, Ativan, T3s, and atropine to dry up the rattle that often developed in the chest shortly before death. In the 1800s we would have been known as a two-woman travelling medicine show.

Amongst the white towels we carried in the trunk were two dark green ones we saved for hemorrhages. Red doesn't show up as easily against green.

I know, if I'm ever in a tight spot, I can always get work as a cabbie. The city is laid out in my head like a grid; I recognize streets by the houses people died in. It is a rare day that I drive through town without seeing myself standing on one of the doorsteps, hand raised, about to knock.

———————

In Tony Kushner's *Angels in America* there is a scene in which Harper Pitt has a vision while looking out the plane window on a night flight to San Francisco:

> *Souls were rising, from the earth far below, souls of the dead, of people who had perished, from famine, from war, from the plague, and they floated up, like skydivers in reverse, limbs all akimbo, wheeling and spinning. And the souls of these departed joined hands, clasped ankles and formed a web, a great net of souls.*

There were nights when it felt as if we were rising along with the dead, clasping each other's ankles, holding on for dear life.

Here and There

In the West we are largely uninstructed about interludes. From *inter* "between" and *ludus* "a play," *interlude* historically referred to the farcical episodes introduced between the acts of long mystery plays. Take it a step further, and is not the interval, the transition between life and death, one of life's ludicrously improbable situations? An interval between the acts of two long mysteries.

With death, wrote P. K. Page, there is a divide between *here* and *there*. Were it not, she noted, for the inconsequential *t*, the words would be identical.

THREE

The Dynamic Corpse

*For all its grave stillness there is nothing more dynamic
than a corpse. It is the event of passage taking
place before our very eyes.*
—ROBERT POGUE HARRISON, *The Dominion of the Dead*

The Body Deserted

In my mother's last year, her world was measured out in small rooms. Confined to her house because of weakness, she went from the living room, where she could look out on the neighbourhood, to the kitchen, where she could make herself tea, to finally being unable to leave her bedroom. After a serious fall, in which the skin between her wrist and elbow was peeled off, leaving her muscles and tendons exposed like one of the human bodies in Gunther von Hagens's travelling Body Worlds show, home support workers came in daily to help. One woman, from the Philippines, arrived in a wedding dress with frills scalloped down the back. Her wedding plans had fallen apart months ago, but she was not about to waste a good dress and was on her way to a dance after settling Mom in for the night. She served tea in her floor-length lace gown and when Colleen, the woman with Down syndrome who had lived with my mother for thirty years, saw this vision, she went upstairs and put on a crown and a pair of gossamer strap-on wings and came downstairs to join the tea party looking like Titania, Queen of the Faeries, only with almond-shaped eyes and a slightly protruding tongue. In the photo my mother took of them, they look weightless, like Chagall angels.

The women who bathed her, made her meals and helped my mother onto a commode in her last weeks were all immigrants. Women whose past lives I had no idea about, who could have been scientists or doctors or engineers in the countries they came from. Without exception, they were kind women. She died in the arms of a home support worker from Iran. She took a sip of tea and handed her cup to Mahvash, who reached out for her as she began falling backwards on her bed. I didn't see it coming. All my years of working with the dying amounted to a hill of beans when it came to my mother's death.

I started out to write that my mother died of old age, but this is not quite right. She died because she was tired. She no longer wanted to live. I was in the business of helping people die, but when it came to my mother I just didn't see it. Two weeks before her death, she told me a woman in a long white dress had come to her in the night. The woman, radiant and strangely familiar, held out her hand in a kind of invitation. My mother wondered if it was her mother coming for her.

It was my job to look death squarely in the face; it was my job not to flinch. She looked me directly in the eye and asked, "Do you think this means I will die soon?" The grief counsellor in me checked right out. "Buck up, buttercup," I said. "You'll be better in no time."

I didn't see the woman in the long white dress. I didn't see that my mother had already reached out her own hand—that she was floating, like one of Chagall's brides, above the earth. "Will God or someone else," wrote the artist, "give me strength to breathe the breath of prayer and mourning into my paintings?"

The call came from my sister, on a Saturday morning, when I was at work. One minute I was a worker, the next a mourner surrounded by the dying. I told the nurse I was working with that my mother had died. She reached out to hold me, but it was an awkward embrace; this death was too close to home for both of us. We switch sides in the blink of an eye. Did I think, in some magical way, that if I hid in plain sight of death it would not find me? Of course I did.

My sister's voice was uncommonly gentle. That should have been a clue. How the news of a death is delivered can have a lasting impression. In B.C., a program called the Death Notification Program was launched in September 2012 to help paramedics understand the right and wrong ways to deliver the traumatic news of someone's death. The instructor tells the first responders to use direct language, to use words such as *dead* or *died*, as opposed to *passed away* or *gone*. He tells them they will become part of the family's history: "Get it right, they'll never forget you. Get it wrong, they'll never forgive you."

After my mother died, I wanted to see her at home, in the room where I'd spoon-fed her wine a few weeks earlier, when she stopped eating solids. The same room she'd converted into a beauty salon and where, in the late fifties, I served sherry to her "victims," as she called them, at ten o'clock on Saturday mornings. I could picture her in her house. If she wasn't there, where in the world could she be? *Corpus*, from the late fourteenth century, refers to "the body of a person" as well as to "a collection of facts or things." In linguistics, it refers to "a body of utterances as words or sentences." My mother was never at a loss for words; she was a consummate storyteller. Like Albert Finney in Tim Burton's film *Big Fish*, the line between fact and myth was never really clear with her. I wanted, in place of silence, a body of utterances. I wanted to hear her side of the story.

When I saw her in the hospital morgue, she was lying on a steel gurney in a half-zipped black body bag in the middle of an empty room. Her face was uncovered and her hands, with their magenta nails, were resting on her chest. Although I have no recollection of it, I'm told I stroked her head and kept repeating, "Oh Mom, what have you gone and done now?" The morgue smelled like an over-chlorinated pool; the viewing room was brightly lit, and along with Patrick, who had come with me, a nurse and a security guard sat in chairs by the door in accordance with policy at Lions Gate Hospital, where the dead cannot be viewed without supervision. I didn't want strangers in the room; it irritated me. Better eight thousand clay soldiers guarding the dead than two uncomfortable hospital employees.

The dead are cold the way something taken out of the fridge is cold—not a surface chill, but a cold that permeates to the core, a cold that feels like stone. There is no yield, no give. It felt as if I was outside myself in the morgue, watching from a distance as I touched my mother's brow. This is my mother, I thought, and at the same time, This is not.

Along with the presence of death, we are shaken by the absence of life: the body deserted. The temporary shelter abandoned. With death, we close up the house, so to speak, turning down the thermostat as our mothers told us to, checking that the lights are off and the iron unplugged. We lock the door when we leave. At the moment of death the muscles relax completely and then stiffen, starting with the eyelids, jaw and neck. Rigor mortis, literally "death stiffness," sets in about three hours after death and gradually dissipates three days later—as if the body steels itself, and then softens, for whatever might be next.

In the West, a body is required, by law, to be transported in a dark, leak-proof plastic bag not unlike one you might get from an upscale dry cleaner when you pick up your suit or evening gown. A few years ago, Native chiefs in northern Manitoba were not impressed during an outbreak of H1N1 influenza when, along with medical supplies, the government shipped body bags to northern reserves. The bags were returned by First Nations leaders to the Health Canada office, where they were dumped on the floor outside the building's lobby. "To prepare for death," says Wasagamack chief Jerry Knott, "is to invite death." I'm pretty sure the chief would not be happy with the current trend of buying designer coffins and using them as coffee tables until the time comes.

Inside the bag, a cardboard toe tag is fastened, with a piece of string, to the body to ensure proper identification. I don't know how or why it became the norm to zip the bag completely up; perhaps it was to protect against disease, perhaps it was to spare the living having to gaze too long upon the corpse. Whatever the reason, I asked the undertaker, who looked like an overdressed delivery boy in an ill-fitting suit, to leave my mother's face uncovered when he zipped up the body bag. He agreed, although reluctantly, as this was against protocol.

When we took her the short distance outside, to the van waiting to take her to the funeral home, it was the first time she had been outside in a year. Rain fell on her cold face. It filled the creeks and swirled in small whirlpools down storm drains. It fell on her the way it fell on Holly Golightly and Cat in *Breakfast at Tiffany's*, and it fell on her the way it had fallen on the attic roof when I was a girl and everywhere water was running, and my mother and I were dry in adjoining beds and full of sleep.

Many Spaniards, mused García Lorca, live indoors until the day they die and are taken out into the sunlight. What instinct compels us to carry the dead out into the sun, to sit with them, to sing to them, to let the rain fall on their uncovered faces? *Move him into the sun—gently its touch awoke him once*, wrote Wilfred Owen. *Think how it wakes the seeds—woke, once, the clays of a cold star.* Do we hope, against all reason, that the sun will warm them one last time? That the rain will wake them?

My mother's last journal entry, dated March 3, 2004, reads *A sunny day, crocus yellow and purple down the side of the garden*. In the tradition of the Japanese poets, it is a perfect death haiku. Her last look around.

Jewish belief holds that the soul of one recently dead has neither left this world nor entered the world to come. In that room with its sterile metal drawers filled with the recent dead, it felt as if my mother's corpse still belonged to her; as if she was giving me time to say goodbye.

Once, at work, when the funeral home was delayed, I sat with a woman's body for the few hours it took for them to come for her. Her room had a monastic feel to it. There was a jar of wildflowers on the windowsill and a book on her side table; other than that, she had given away her possessions. She lay on a narrow bed, beneath a light blanket, with her face uncovered. At one point it occurred to me that although there were two of us in the room, I was the only one breathing. I felt each breath in a way I never had before; aware of how the air I was breathing in was cool and how, when it left my body, it was warm. *Inspire*, from the Latin *in* "in" and *spirare* "to breathe," has the same etymology as *inspiration* — "immediate influence of God or a god." Every breath we take in is sacred. *Exhale*, from the Latin *exhalare*, means "to breathe out, evaporate." Within days of our final exhalation, we vanish. Although how completely is questionable, at least to physicist Enrico Fermi, who calculated that with a single breath we breathe in a single molecule from Caesar's last exhalation.

The Danish poet Ulrikka Gernes, a good friend, told Patrick that when she gave her father, Poul, mouth-to-mouth resuscitation shortly before he died, she realized, just before she stopped, that the only air in her father's lungs was her own. It was her breath, making small bubbling sounds, that he breathed out with his last breath.

When his father was dying, Patrick matched him breath for breath. There was a moment when it struck him that his father wasn't going to take a breath in, and he thought, I'm going to have to. His poem "standing the night through," written shortly after his father's death, starts with the lines

> *like jesus' death*
> *pa's death split everything into before and after*
> *and nothing was healed.*

The silence in the patient's room was that of *before* and *after*. Death's demarcation line. I watched the light move slowly across the room, inching its way up her body as if anointing her. When we sit for one, do we sit for the others in our lives for whom this was not possible—the ones my mother lost in the war? my brother? my mother? the ones with nobody to bury them? Do we tell the nurse to leave us alone when she comes to take the body away, as Patrick did after his father died, so that he could talk to him and wash the sleep from his eyes with a cool face cloth? Is there an interval, a pause, an amount of time between two states, when they might still hear us? Does the spirit linger for itself? Not for us, although maybe that too. What do we sit with when we sit with the dead? We sit, do we not, gobsmacked at the mystery of it all.

On Dead People's Heads

In 1951, archaeologist Dr. Ralph Solecki set up camp in the rock-strewn hills outside the Shanidar Cave in northern Iraq's Zagros Mountains, 2,500 feet above sea level. The Kurdish goatherds and their families who live in the cave from November to April have built individual brush huts inside it, each with a small fireplace and corrals for goats, chickens, cows and horses. From the mouth one can see the Great Zab River, a tributary of the Tigris, glistening off in the distance. In four field seasons, lasting until 1960, Solecki and his team from Columbia University dug, swept and chipped their way through limestone layers to the Neanderthal skeletons below. Of the nine they unearthed, one, Shanidar IV, was found to be lying on the remnants of woody branches and brightly coloured wildflowers.

Were these first burials evidence of love, or were they as simple a thing as an idea of beauty? Patrick and I disagree about love. He believes there was a time in human history when we were animal with a glimmering and growing consciousness; a time when survival trumped everything. He doesn't deny the existence of an early bond between people; he just doesn't think it was love as we know it. I can't imagine a time before love.

Whatever our differences, we both agree that something shifted in human consciousness around the time Nandy, as the Neanderthal was affectionately known, was laid to rest on a bed of yellow yarrow, common groundsel, woody horsetail, grape hyacinth, hollyhocks and St. Barnaby's thistle.

A hand scattering petals eighty thousand years ago is a hand scattering petals over the little bird graves in my mother's backyard fifty years ago. An impulse. An offering. Not to the gods necessarily, not for good luck or safe travel or prosperity. We fly, as Emerson wrote in his journal, "we fly to beauty as an asylum from the terrors of finite nature."

In the home of a Second World War veteran dying of brain cancer, I noticed an exquisite wall hanging beside his bed. Imprisoned for three years in a Japanese prisoner of war camp, he had pulled single threads from his uniform and woven them into a tapestry. He embroidered green mountains and footbridges over deep blue pools. He wove ducks sleeping under willow trees and great white cranes lifting off the ground with their black legs dangling helplessly. He did not weave the fields of grain from his home in Saskatchewan nor the crow or blackbird on the reed; he didn't embroider train tracks cutting across fields of snow or smoke threading its way lazily out of a chimney. He took refuge in what was in front of him, beyond the barbed wire, in the madhouse of beauty.

We open our hands and let fall the blossoms.

It's all guesswork. Joseph Campbell believed that the first burials implied a recognition of the cycle of life. From our agrarian roots, he imagined bodies planted in the earth like seed pods. A variation of the pods in the fictional town of Santa Mira, California, where the townspeople were replaced by perfect physical duplicates, simulacrums grown from giant pods in the 1956 film *The Invasion of the Body Snatchers*. Reverence and horror are close companions in the kingdom of death and dying.

Of all the quandaries having to do with death, the most obvious continues to be what to do with the body. From the first intentional burials, at which goods were placed in the graves of our ancestors in preparation for the afterlife, to the fetuses kept in glass jars for scientific research, we have a responsibility to our dead. We bury, believes Robert Pogue Harrison, "not simply to achieve closure and effect a separation from the dead but also and above all to humanize the ground on which we build our worlds." Over the centuries we have lost track of where people are buried: we have built villages and cities on top of long-forgotten burial grounds and bulldozed ancient grave sites to build townhouses and golf courses. The most serious armed standoff between First

Nations and "mainstream" Canadian society in modern times was over a golf course planned for a Native burial ground at Oka, Quebec. When paleontologists re-excavated the Combe Grenal cave in France, from 1953 to 1965, they unearthed sixty different layers of human occupation. Under a suburb in St. Louis, archaeologists found thirteen settlements on top of each other. We live, as Annie Dillard says, "on dead people's heads."

In the fifth century BC, the Greek philosopher Empedocles posited that all matter was composed of four elements. The building blocks of life were once believed to be fire, water, air and earth—the same elements into which we relinquish our dead. If ancient philosophers believed that all things were formed from these four elements, the modern philosopher does not agree. The periodic table tells us we are made up of thirty elements, but in our imaginations and our creation myths we are created from the elemental: a god's tears, clay, Athena's breath, fire and ice.

Fire

As humans, we have a primal relationship with fire. It warms us and feeds us and wards off wolves howling in the night. We sit in the dark, our faces lit by flames, and tell each other ghost stories. When I was a young girl, I spent hours striking two stones together over a bundle of dry grass trying to get a spark the way I'd seen cowboys do it in the movies. We fight fire with fire, literally lighting backfires to deprive large fires of fuel; birds rise out of its ashes; we have fire in our bellies;

there are fire-eaters and fire-walkers; and it is rumoured that some people have spontaneously burst into flame and burned like human candles until nothing was left. It is destruction and creation: the funeral pyre and the volcano.

Fire is the great transformer—taking material from this world and delivering it like a takeout order to the next. It is white, red, yellow, orange and blue, and when a human body is placed in it, it consumes the remains like an animal with an insatiable appetite.

In Varanasi, a city situated on the banks of the Ganges River in Uttar Pradesh, the Manikarnika Ghat performs four hundred cremations a day. When my son, Saul, was nineteen and travelling in India, he wrote to me saying that Varanasi was the undisputed king of all things associated with that country—sadhus, Buddhists, beggars, movies, slums and heat. He watched the body of his yoga instructor burn on the banks of the Ganges in Rishikesh. It takes three to four hours for a body, smeared with clarified butter, to burn, within which time it is hoped the skull will explode to release the soul from the flesh, allowing reincarnation or ascension to heaven. If it doesn't, it's smashed with a stick, ensuring the soul is released. Kailash Choudhari is a boatman and member of the Dome caste in Varanasi; every member of his family has lived and died on the burning ghats. "We were raised to work the fires," says Choudhari. "Without our fire ceremony, dead bodies could not burn in the proper way." Known as "the lords of this earth," he and his family often see souls dancing in the flames. On the roads leading to Varanasi it is not unusual to see shrouded corpses strapped like kayaks or surfboards to the roofs of vehicles on their way to the river.

Why is it that trivia catches my attention? Da Vinci believed the heart was of such density that fire could scarcely destroy it. Not so. Of the bodies that are cremated, often a man's chest bone and a woman's hips will not burn completely. We go through our lives with places in our bodies capable of withstanding fire. Our hearts go up in flames every time. Choudhari once saw a burning body stand up to speak, but no words came out when it opened its mouth. The bones that don't burn are deposited in the Ganges along with the fifty or so bodies a day that can't be cremated—those of holy men, children, pregnant women, lepers and people who die of snakebite.

"A human limb burns a little like a tree branch," says fire investigator John DeHaan. For a few minutes, in the stainless steel vault of a crematorium preheated to eleven hundred degrees Fahrenheit, we ignite like tinder-dry saplings.

Water
The human body is made up of over 60 percent water. We come from water, say the evolutionists, and some of us return to it. New research suggests that our gills are still sitting in our throats—disguised as our parathyroid glands. For Christians, baptism symbolizes death by water and rebirth; you "drown," whether by being submerged or having a few drops of water sprinkled over your head, and surface as a new person. We live for nine months in the watery home of our mother's womb and arrive in the world when the waters break. Without water, we are dead in five to seven days. It flows from one place to another; it originates from a source

that is often hidden from us and carves pathways through stone; it is blessing and curse. Ancient Norsemen, believing that water had the power to restore life, sent the bodies of their heroes out to sea in "death ships" in the hope they would return to them once again. As children, we fall asleep imagining lost underwater continents peopled with creatures who are part human, part fish.

In Canada, the disposal of human remains at sea is regulated under the Canadian Environmental Protection Act, Part VI. The long and the short of it is that the burial of bodies at sea is not a thing to be encouraged. It is one thing to scatter ashes on the water, quite another to release a corpse into Davy Jones's underwater locker. Legend has it that Davy Jones was either an incompetent sailor or a pub owner who kidnapped sailors. Some also think he was Satan or Jonah, the devil of the seas. One of the concerns about burial at sea is that the body will be hauled up by a fishing boat. In order to avoid this, anyone wishing to go this watery route must first pay a $2,500 application fee to the Receiver General of Canada and put a notice of intent in the local newspaper. To top it off, the casket must be weighted with iron and steel and have a concrete mix placed at the foot of the corpse. The coffin must then be drilled full of holes. Even Houdini would be stumped.

For Canada's servicemen and -women at sea, it is less problematic. Because of a lack of coffins on board, the body is placed in a burial shroud, weighted with rocks, or sometimes cannonballs, and released into the depths.

Of all the rules, regulations and procedures I encountered, the thing that surprised me the most was the fact that cannonballs still exist.

Water is a pathway and a purifier. On days when I felt myself saturated with death, my mother-in-law, Rose, told me to go to a river or swiftly running creek and brush myself off with cedar. The few times I did this, I invariably felt lighter, as if the dead let go of me or were washed away in the clear, cold water.

It is said that ghosts travel from one place to another on underground streams.

I have stood on the spit near the mouth of the Capilano River and shown my children where I want my ashes scattered: at the place where sea water and fresh water mingle. Freighters regularly pass nearby under Lions Gate Bridge, and the lights of the city form a second city on the water's surface. I will live in this second city, along with my mother and John, whose ashes were released there long ago.

In her poem "Water," Gwendolyn MacEwen might as easily have been writing about death itself:

> When you think of it, water is everything. Or rather
> Water ventures into everything and becomes everything.
> > It has
> All tastes and moods imaginable; water is history
> And the end of the world is water also.

When we give up our dead to the water—as ash or corpse—we give them up to the peripatetic movements of the currents. They become travellers, sojourners, voyageurs beneath the dark, impenetrable sea.

Air

Of all the elements, air seems the most mysterious to me. It has neither shape nor colour nor smell; it is everywhere and yet it is invisible to us. It is the domain of spirit: of winged creatures, real and imagined—vultures and angels—and it is the playground of the gods. Without it, there is no life. When we speak of air, we speak of the earth's atmosphere—the clear gas, made up mainly of oxygen and nitrogen—in which we live and breathe. Our last act on earth is to breathe out the air in our lungs. Air is movement and imagination, revealing itself by what it touches, as Christina Rossetti wrote:

> *Who has seen the wind?*
> *Neither I nor you:*
> *But when the leaves hang trembling,*
> *The wind is passing through.*

And—it is the place of miraculous burials.

In the West, we avoid touching bodies; that work is left to morticians. The thought of cutting a corpse into bite-sized pieces and pulverizing the bones is, to the Western mind, the stuff of horror films. To the Tibetans, it is spiritual practice. Sky burials, or *jhator* as they are otherwise known, are considered an act of generosity on the part of the deceased, who essentially offer themselves up as part of the food chain. *Jhator*, meaning "giving alms to the birds," generally takes place on a large flat rock on a high ridge at dawn. On the day of the funeral, the body, which has been wrapped in a white blanket and prayed over by monks for days, is carried by a family member to the door of the house of the *rogyapa*, or "body breaker," who then carries it on his back to the rock platform, where he dismembers it, scattering bits of flesh and organs to the vultures and carrion birds waiting nearby. He then smashes the bones and mixes them with flour and butter for the hawks and smaller birds to eat, until there is nothing left of the body. The corpse must be completely disposed of so that the soul is free to leave it.

As I write this, the nights are getting longer and the air cooler. I am in a cabin in the woods and the night scavengers are hard at work. *Scavenger*, from the Middle English *scawageour*, originally referred to "a person hired to remove refuse from the streets." The street cleaners of today are vultures, blowflies, yellow jackets, burying beetles, owls, raccoons and crows. Although the concept of air burial is foreign to the West, if we stop and think about it, we are living in the midst of such burials all the time. A couple of days ago a bird hit the sliding glass window at my house; it was clear, from the angle of its neck, that it had died instantly. I meant to bury it but forgot until the next morning, when I went looking for the body. It was gone. Aside from the mark on the window, there was no proof that there had even been a bird. We carry on, oblivious to the bones cracking and little souls rising all around us, every moment of the day and night.

On the highest mountain, in the highest graveyard in the world, the bodies of mountain climbers lie frozen on the slopes. There are over two hundred bodies on Mount Everest, making it one of the world's few open graveyards. The living walk amongst the strange sculptures of the unreachable dead. For years, the body of Hannelore Schmatz could be seen sitting upright, leaning against her pack, with her eyes open and hair blowing in the wind. The winds are constant and unpredictable. At a border crossing high in the Andes between Chile and Argentina, I marvelled at the wind-sculpted seashell patterns that fanned out from the base of the mountains like the trains of wedding gowns. A Sherpa who tried to recover Hannelore's body in 1984 fell to his death, along with another rescuer, and finally it was the high, sculpting winds that blew her remains over the edge and down the Kangshung Face.

Prior to contact with the Europeans, a number of First Nations on the West Coast placed their dead in open caskets in treetops. In Haida Gwaii, the bodies of high-ranking chiefs were placed inside mortuary poles with the belief that if the physical body was lifted up, the spirit would be set free. Years ago, I asked my ex-husband what he wanted done with his body in the event of his death. "Put me in a tree," he said.

Thanks a lot, I thought. That oughta be easy.

Earth

The phrase *six feet under* originated in England in 1665, when the death rate from the bubonic plague reached seven thousand per week. The mayor of London issued a decree that all bodies must be buried six feet underground in order to help stop the spread of infection. Of course, it was later discovered that the plague was spread by fleas from rats, and the only thing that stopped the disease was the Great Fire of London in 1666, which effectively wiped out all the rats.

In addition to holding tree burials, the Salish constructed cairns beneath which the body was placed in a shallow grave lined with stones. Later, when these burial practices were outlawed, the elders were said to be distraught at the thought of the spirit having to dig its way out from under six feet of dirt. My mother, too, was distraught at the thought of her son so far underground.

There are graveyards everywhere. In the middle of an old-growth forest on Haida Gwaii, I came across moss-covered tombstones that were sinking into the earth. The inscription on Chief Skedan's headstone, dated 1890, reads, "He tried to be a Christian." Right around the time he was trying his best, a census by the Hudson's Bay Company estimated that 95 percent of the Haida population had been wiped out by disease following first contact. By 1915, the population had dropped from 30,000 to 588. The chief would have grasped the idea of a wrathful God with no problem; it was the concept of a merciful one that must have caused him no end of trouble.

The earth is always giving up little treasures: plastic horses, Dinky Toys, marbles, coins, odd bones, buttons, arrowheads, tarnished spoons and rusty metal soldiers. It is the boneyard of our childhood. In the backyard of the home I grew up in are four cats in shoeboxes, numerous birds in holes lined with grass, and something—I can't remember what—in a matchbox.

On the prairies, family plots are often hidden by tall grasses. Patrick's grandmother is buried in one of them somewhere near Blumenort, "the place of flowers." These graves feel as if they hold the history of this country, from the unmarked white crosses grouped like clumps of wild daisies in empty fields where family farms once thrived, to the churchyards that buried local people close to home. Bodies are seeded in the land in forgotten cemeteries where wooden fences have fallen down and markers are long gone. How can we not think, standing in an open field, of the multitudinous dead beneath our feet and of the problems this potentially raises in terms of real estate. In 1914, San Francisco passed an ordinance forbidding further burials and evicted the dead from local cemeteries located on prime land. Bodies were relocated to the south, to Colma, a city with an area of 2.2 square miles on which seventeen cemeteries are housed. Colma, or the City of Souls as it is known, has a population of 1,500 above ground and 1.5 million underground.

In the heat of a summer day, the earth gives up its hiding places; a pervasive stench alerts us to an animal's death. We sense the visible evidence of the thousands upon thousands of invisible things that live and die amongst us every moment of the day. For some, the smell of death is repellent; for others, it is an elixir. Along the northern gas pipelines, engineers trying to figure out where there are leaks pump in the smell of decaying meat and wait for the turkey vultures to gather. Without fail, the birds of prey zero in on every leak every time. In South Africa, flies are attracted to orchids that mimic the smell of carrion. The smell of death, it would seem, is sometimes intricately linked to the art of deception.

A few years ago, when I went with my daughters to Chile, we drove around the Cementerio General de Santiago in the back of a beat-up van listening to U2 on the radio singing about forgiveness and raising the dead. When babies die in Chile, they are buried with a pair of white wings, made from chicken feathers glued onto a cardboard base. The babies, not having committed any sins, are thought to be *angelitos* and the wings, attached with elastic bands, help them fly straight to heaven. In 1992, the bodies of Pablo Neruda and his wife, Matilde Urrutia, were dug up from the cemetery and reburied at their home on Isla Negra. In 1926, he wrote,

> *There are cemeteries that are lonely,*
> *graves full of bones that do not make a sound,*
> *the heart moving through a tunnel,*
> *in it darkness, darkness, darkness . . .*
> *death is inside the bones,*
> *like a barking where there are no dogs.*

———————

One day not long ago, I went with my youngest daughter, Salia, and her dad, Floyd, to a small graveyard in North Vancouver. Located on an urban reserve, Eslhá7an, or the Mission Reserve, is a resting place for city ghosts. Just down the dirt road, St. Paul's Indian Church sits on the inlet a few yards from where the canoes used to pull up. At night, the two blue neon crosses on top of the church spires light up like freshly cracked Glow Sticks and can be seen by the skiers on top of Grouse Mountain. We passed beneath a carved cedar canoe suspended over the entrance and made our way, as my daughter commented, "into a sea of crosses."

The graveyard holds the stories, the history, lost languages, songs; it holds the hereditary chiefs and the elected, the Indian dancers and the Christians. It holds the body of Floyd's seventeen-year-old brother, Ben, who drowned one summer day when he jumped off the silver train bridge, yelling

"Geronimo," and never came back up. It holds the memory of his mother, Rose, throwing herself on his grave every night and sleeping there until morning, when Floyd would come and bring her home.

It holds the name of the elder who welcomed Captain George Vancouver into Burrard Inlet on June 13, 1792, when the mud flats were rich with clams and salmon climbed out of the river as men.

One thing it doesn't hold is the body of Floyd's great-grandfather, Chief Moses. When the Church wanted to appropriate more land for its own uses, Moses refused. The bishop made good on his promise and the chief was buried somewhere outside the cemetery, without a marker.

Many burial parks now offer "natural" or "green" burials at which unembalmed bodies, clothed or wrapped in bio-degradable garments, are placed in caskets made of wicker, recycled cardboard or natural fibre and buried in unmarked graves, where they decompose naturally and become part of the natural landscape. Damp, rich soil—containing billions of soil organisms—will reduce an unembalmed corpse to bones in just nine months. A perfect gestation. On a list of burial options ranging from elaborate to the very basic, it is now possible, in a number of places, to choose composting.

I am a relatively new gardener with the zealous commitment of an ex-smoker. I love how the things we compost break down and feed the garden. I have trouble, though, with the red wigglers—the workers of rot. As Voltaire observes,

To numerous insects shall my corpse give birth,
When once it mixes with its mother earth:
Small comfort 'tis that when Death's ruthless power
Closes my life, worms shall my flesh devour.

Bears, wolves and eagles drag salmon from streams into the forest, where the nitrogen-rich remains of the fish fertilize the flora. The ancient forests of the Pacific Northwest grow tall on the blood and flesh of fish. The great canopies are fertilized by the dead.

My brother has been underground for half a century. What, then, of him lives in the verdant green grass and wildflowers that grow above his grave?

Ashes

In North America, we don't know what to do with our dead. We call the cremated remains of our loved ones *cremains*, which, to my way of thinking, sounds far too much like *Craisins* to be taken seriously. We plant trees and engrave the names of our loved ones on memorial benches overlooking the ocean; we gather as families to scatter the ashes but are not quite prepared for their weight and texture, or for the way the wind doesn't disperse them as we had imagined. In movies, human ashes seem more like stardust—the bright dust in the night sky we imagined as children.

The reality is somewhat different. In *The Big Lebowski*, Jeff Bridges ends up covered in Donny's ashes when the wind, off the Pacific, whips them backwards just as John Goodman intones, "Goodbye, sweet prince," and pours them out of a Folgers coffee tin. When we scattered my mother's ashes off the dock in front of the Cannery Seafood Restaurant on Burrard Inlet, they didn't lift in an ethereal manner; rather, they turned a luminescent green as they sank and swirled downwards. It appeared to me as if my mother had turned into a fish and left us abruptly with a flash of her new emerald scales.

My mother loved the Cannery. She loved sitting at a window table with a carafe of white wine and watching the working harbour: the freighters loading and unloading cargo, the Cates tugs, and Seaspan barges with pyramids of sawdust piled on their decks. She watched the orange SeaBus scuttling between North Van and the city, and she waited, every time, to see Ralph, the massive sea lion who hung around the restaurant waiting for scraps. When she told me she wanted her ashes scattered off the dock, she said, "Don't worry, I'm sure I'll end up inside of Ralph." A thought which seemed to amuse her no end.

Some of us are more pragmatic than others. Herodotus tells us that the Callatians ate their dead as a way of honouring them. Queen Artemisia is said to have mixed the ashes of her beloved with wine and drunk them. One woman, a potter, whose father died at hospice, mixed his ashes into wet clay and shaped him into a set of coffee mugs.

In modern Japan, where cremation is predominant, it is common for the close relatives of the deceased to remove the bones from the ashes with chopsticks. In her essay "Letter from a Japanese Crematorium," Marie Mutsuki Mockett describes how her uncle and grandfather picked her grandmother's bones out of the ashes stretched out on a steel table. "They started with the feet first so my grandmother would not be upside down in her rectangular urn." An attendant in the background identified each bone. "Here is the second joint of the big toe. Here is a fragment of the femur." The last pieces of bone to be placed in the urn were those of the skull and jaw, and the hyoid bone, from the Adam's apple, which rests in a separate box. This is the only time that two people will hold anything together using chopsticks, Mockett says, "hence the reason the Japanese flinch if two people inadvertently reach down to pick up the same morsel of food from a plate."

Cremation in North America is a two-step process. First the body is burned for several hours, after which the dry bone fragments are swept out of the incinerator and pulverized by a bone crusher until they look like grains of sand. We do not pick out bone fragments or place the ashes feet first in urns; we want fire, with its voracious appetite, to transform flesh and bone to dust.

Pacemakers have to be removed before cremation, as they can explode. Tooth fillings are sometimes buried in consecrated ground, sometimes sold as scrap metal.

Keith Richards claims that he snorted his father's ashes mixed with a bit of cocaine: "The strangest thing I've tried to snort? My father. I snorted my father," Richards was quoted as saying by British music magazine *NME*. Hunter S. Thompson's ashes were shot from a very large cannon placed atop a 153-foot tower in Colorado to the tune of Bob Dylan's "Mr. Tambourine Man." Go online and you'll find no shortage of things made from human ashes: pencils, photographs, diamonds, sculptures, vinyl records, glass beads, and ink for tattoos for those who want to wear their loved ones on their skin. Three miles off Key Largo, the Atlantis Reef, an underwater mausoleum made of human ashes mixed with concrete, stretches across sixteen acres of ocean floor. Brightly coloured fish dart in and out of the sculptures of this sunken city just the way they did in the castle in my fish tank when I was a child.

When my mother died, a friend, Louie John, offered to sit with her body the night before the funeral. The funeral director said that would be impossible. "We'd have to hire a security guard," she said. "We can't just have somebody sitting here all night." A guard to watch over the man watching over the dead. I should have insisted. The bereaved are weak. I was acquiescent in my sorrow, compliant in my grief.

I wish I had accompanied my mother's casket to the crematorium, maybe even pushed the button to open the heavy door of the fiery vault. I was afraid to see her body consumed by fire, to see her disappear so completely. I left her in the chapel in her casket. I don't know where she went or who took her there. It's not rational to think I let her down, but then grief is not rational. Sometimes we need permission or direction—someone to take baby steps with us. Someone to say, Have you thought of *this*, have you thought of *that*?

If, as the Israeli poet Yehuda Amichai believed, the air above Jerusalem was heavy with prayers, then surely the air we breathe must be saturated with the dead. Over one million pounds of human ashes are produced every day: four pounds of ash per human female and six pounds per human male. It's amazing we aren't knee-deep in ash.

In British Columbia the rate of cremation is 80 percent—the highest in Canada—and, remarkably, 5 percent of the ashes are never claimed.

I phone Lorraine Fracy at Royal Oak Burial Park in Victoria to ask what happens to those ashes. Lorraine's background is in physical education. When she was twenty-eight, she was running a women's fitness club but feeling that something was missing. When her sister, a funeral director, asked her to help out with the funeral of a young man, Lorraine thought, Why not? and ended up standing beside the open casket as the mourners filed past. It was as if she'd come home. She remembers bowing her head as a child and saying a prayer whenever a funeral procession passed by, and she says it was this respect for the dead that led her to become a funeral director and cemeterian.

"It's the elephant in the room," Lorraine tells me.

When I ask her what she means, she explains that there

are unclaimed urns in funeral homes all over the city. In 2001, when Lorraine started working at the burial park, there were 125 unclaimed remains. I'm confounded by this. How, I wonder, could people not pick up their relatives? Over the years, she tracked down families—some of whom didn't know where the ashes were, some who had estranged relationships and didn't want the ashes, a few who said, "Flush them."

"For some people," she says, "grief is just too raw and they can't face it." There are now forty urns remaining, and no leads left to family members.

Some of the urns in her care were brought to her by strangers in the community who just happened to find them. One man found an urn in a dryer he bought at a used-appliance store; another found a container of ashes on a city bench. There are others, Lorraine tells me, who ask how much money it would cost to put the ashes in the ground on top of an existing grave, and who balk when they find out there is a minimal fee for someone to lift the sod and place the ashes in the grave. "It's not unusual," she says, "to find ashes dumped on top of graves." What people don't think about is how leaf blowers or lawn mowers will disperse them in a matter of seconds.

Ashes, it seems, point to the complexities of human relationships and the complications of grief.

There are others, she notes, who are extraordinarily attentive and for whom the cremated remains of their loved ones are precious. On a very basic level, it is about respect.

Having unclaimed remains sitting on a shelf in a funeral

home, to some cultures, would mean their loved one is not at peace. First Nations people have spent decades recovering the bones of their ancestors from museums around the world, and, Lorraine tells me, in recent years a number of Japanese people have approached her about how to go about retrieving the bodies of family members who are interred in graveyards that are now being bulldozed in order to build shopping malls. She will not rest until the ashes in her care are properly buried, and she says that, in the near future, the remains from the forty urns will be placed in an unrecoverable, unmarked grave. She will have a simple ceremony to lay to rest the ashes that nobody wants.

We hedge our bets. If there is an afterlife, we'd best get there well equipped. Early Upper Paleolithic burial sites contained necklaces, bracelets, hunting weapons, and objects made of animal teeth. Some bodies were buried with tools, others with ornaments made of shells and stone beads—grave goods, as they are known.

Oh, build your ship of death, instructed D. H. Lawrence, *your little ark / and furnish it with food, with little cakes, and wine / for the dark flight down oblivion.*

We filled my mother's little ark with a fair share of grave goods: letters, books, poems, CDs, Werther's candies in gold wrappers, a medal on a ribbon, a beaded eagle feather, Shakespeare's twenty-ninth sonnet, a flask of cognac and other things I have forgotten. All reduced to ash, and all four pounds poured into an urn no bigger than a Venti latte from Starbucks. Outside the funeral home, steam rose off the horses' coats; a little farther up the canyon, the river was thundering through the narrow walls. Only later did I realize her casket had been made of cardboard. I hadn't thought to ask them to put her in a plain one made of pine. I wish I had.

MY BROTHER IS BURIED IN THE NORTH VANCOUVER CEMETERY *not far from a wildlife refuge at the foot of Grouse Mountain. The white wolves who roam there—retirees from the movie industry—can be heard howling in the city on cold nights when sound travels with a sharp clarity. Not long ago, quite by accident, I found out that the husband of a good friend of mine had attended UBC in the early sixties and that not only had he known my brother, but he also knew of a friend who had helped with the funeral arrangements.*

There is a genteel, almost a mannered sound to the words the arrangements. *Take out* the *and put* funeral *in front and one can imagine a kind of hushed solemnity. Think again. The etymology of* arrangement, *from the Old French* arengier *(twelfth century), is "to draw a line of battle," from a "to" and* rangier *"set in a row." The battle lines were drawn in the living room filled with white lilies while I played horses in the basement.*

It wasn't until I spoke to Gary, the friend, that I understood what the battle lines were.

Dee, he told me, wanted Ian's body buried and my mother wanted him cremated after a small service at the local parish church. He told me that Dee had called him and asked him to stand with her against my mother. "There will be no service," she said.

"It was a rainy day," he recalled. "We all stood around a gaping hole in the ground. Nobody said a word." There was no mention of God or Allah, Buddha or Krishna. There was no service. "Nobody knew what to do." When there is no outlet, no way to speak, mourning goes underground. It moves along those same streams that ghosts are said to travel on.

I don't know how to think about this—the adamance of it, the intransigence; the pigheadedness of it. All I can think of—the only sense I can make of this—is that it was a time of change, a transition. You must change your life, *wrote Rilke in "Archaic Torso of Apollo." Of course, this is true; and yet, when great change happens, when the old order is breaking down and the new one is not yet defined, what do we do in the space between? When the religiosity of the past no longer works at the graveside, when sermons fail to move us and the business of death knows nothing of the spirit, what do we do?*

Ian died shortly after Jessica Mitford exposed the funeral industry in The American Way of Death. *Traditional ceremonies no longer made sense. It was a time of protest: against war, poverty, racism, religion and "the Establishment." What could theology say about death in an age when the question* Is God Dead? *was about to be emblazoned in large black letters against a red background on the cover of* Time *magazine?*

Two weeks after the accident, my sister, Carol, was married. Our mother, barely in this world, put on a black and white polka-dot dress, short white gloves, nylons and heels and took me with her to City Hall. After the brief ceremony, we went back with my sister and her husband to their friend's house on Fourth Avenue, where the air was thick with the sweet scent of dope and people were sitting around on the floor. Someone gave my sister a joint, inside a roll of Life Savers, which she smoked for breakfast the next morning. The mantra of the sixties, "God is love," had no answer for tragedy. My mother stayed for a little while and then she excused us and we caught a bus at the corner and went home.

When neither the funeral nor the wedding is recognizable to you—how grieve? how celebrate?

The legacy for my mother was one of pain. The lingering grief of nothing mentioned. The importance of ritual, of pausing to acknowledge the magnitude of death, the small kindnesses that are meant to visit one in times of loss—all were absent. We use the words grief *and* mourning *interchangeably—thinking they are the same. They are not. Grief is what the bereaved feel inside; mourning is the expression of those thoughts and feelings. The silence we lived with was the silence of the void. There was no healing, no movement. There was no crack like the sound a frozen river makes when it starts to run. We were frozen in grief.*

How, I wonder, do we hold on to things of value as we change? It would have been good if someone had spoken that day. A few words. Maybe a few lines from his favourite poem by Shakespeare:

> Fear no more the lightning flash,
> Nor the all-dreaded thunder-stone . . .
> All lovers young, all lovers must
> Consign to thee, and come to dust.

Maybe someone could have told a story about him and someone else given a drunken toast. Maybe the wolves could have started up, calling out to each other, as the blue casket was lowered slowly into the muddy hole in the ground.

And then it would have been all right to be silent. It would have been just fine.

Gloria Dei

I once attended a funeral at which the mourners got into their cars, turned on their headlights and followed the hearse as it wound through the town carrying the body of a friend. We drove slowly along the streets he had played on as a child, past the house he was born in, over the railway tracks and past his favourite bar. It was a glorious winter day. The sun was out and the late-winter steelhead were on their way upriver. It was his favourite time of year. We drove along ordinary streets in ordinary neighbourhoods. A boy pedalled his bike beside us, people waved; it was as if we were on parade. My friend was having a last look around and we were his eyes.

There were police cars at the main intersections and constables waving the procession through the red lights. Death was passing like a long freight train. *Because I could not stop for death*, wrote Dickinson, *he kindly stopped for me*. Traffic backed up on either side of the road. There was nothing for the drivers to do but sit and wait.

I will teach you my townspeople / how to perform a funeral, wrote William Carlos Williams in 1916:

> See! the hearse leads.
> I begin with a design for a hearse.
> For Christ's sake not black—
> nor white either—and not polished!
> Let it be weathered—like a farm wagon—
> with gilt wheels (this could be
> applied fresh at small expense)

or no wheels at all:
a rough dray to drag over the ground.

We do not see funeral processions as frequently today as we did in the past. Along with a decline in traditional religious practice, we have fewer rituals with which to express grief; fewer ways to acknowledge death. In small towns it may still be possible to see a procession pass by. However, in cities, where we're largely anonymous to each other, it is harder to see visible evidence of mourning—the funeral coach or the farm wagon—although sometimes the procession simply takes another form.

My friend Claudia, whose brother died in an accident when he was twenty-six, told me the image of my brother crossing the country in a blue casket has merged with the memory of her brother's coffin being escorted by what seemed like the entire contingent of the Squamish Hells Angels, "a slow motorcycle cavalcade from Gloria Dei along the Upper Levels to the cemetery on the hill." It was, she said, an odd, deeply reassuring, unexpected and terribly funny moment. "He wasn't an Angel," says Claudia. "He had some kind of honorary status—maybe they loved his smartass sense of humour, his fringed leather jacket, his Dayton boots which lent him a couple of much-needed inches." Her father, who she was sure was going to follow her brother into the grave that day, not only took the presence of this revving multitude well, but felt the magnitude of the honour along with all who had gathered. "The sheer noise, the massed chorus of bikes and the enormous number of ferocious-looking men did, in that moment, and for the rest of our lives, counterbalance and give voice to the immensity of pain we all felt." Who amongst us would not want the multitudes assembled and revving their choppers in a massed chorus at our passing?

Funerals serve to separate the dead from the living, and the funeral cortège, starting from a church or funeral home and ending up at the cemetery or crematorium, is visible evidence of this symbolic transition. *Procession*, derived from the Latin *processionem*, means "a marching onward"; *cortège*, a word we use interchangeably with *procession*, comes from the Old French *cortège* and refers to "a train of attendants." Before there were cars or motorized funeral coaches, the casket was carried in a horse-drawn carriage, behind which the mourners walked. Sometimes it's even simpler than that. After a formal funeral service is held in St. Paul's, on the Mission Reserve, the men of the community form a line from the church steps to the cemetery five hundred yards down the road. They carry the coffin a short distance and then hand it over to the next group, who carry it before handing it to the next in line. The rest of the mourners—men, women and children—walk slowly behind the casket as it makes its way to the graveyard. The kind of walk Williams might have taken.

> *Then briefly as to yourselves:*
> *Walk behind—as they do in France,*
> *seventh class, or if you ride*
> *Hell take curtains! Go with some show*
> *of inconvenience; sit openly—*
> *to the weather as to grief.*
> *Or do you think you can shut grief in?*

What—from us? We who have perhaps
nothing to lose? Share with us
share with us—it will be money
in your pockets.

I once made this walk in winter; the wind was howling and snow was shifting in whirlpools along the ground and blowing in my eyes. Trees thrashed all around us, but like the eye of a hurricane, inside the cemetery was completely silent and still. For a short while the world was quiet and then, of course, we all walked back into the raging wind.

Cemeterian and Royal Oak Burial Park client supervisor Lorraine Fracy remembers the day, in the mid-1990s, when she realized respect for the dead was no longer what it had been. It was a warm spring day and she was carrying the body of a nineteen-year-old girl to the burial ground in a long black hearse. She nosed the coach out into the traffic and stopped a few inches into a crosswalk when the light turned yellow. A man in a three-piece suit gave her the finger as he walked around the front of her car. At that moment she thought to herself, Respect for the dead is null and void.

We are poorer in the West for our lack of ritual, for what we have forgotten about a shared grief—for thinking we can shut it in. In the past, priests were our practitioners of loss; we now have celebrants legally authorized to conduct weddings and funerals. Boomers, having written their own wedding vows and birthing ceremonies, are now creating their own funeral traditions. The trend is towards celebrating a life as opposed to mourning a death. It's as if we fear the rawness of grief, caught between the Latin *celebrare* "to sing someone's praises" and the Germanic *murnan* "to remember sorrowfully." Ceremonies are conducted in back-yards, yacht clubs, hotels and golf courses. Like the funerals I held in my mother's garden, these ones too could be confused with weddings. The emphasis on celebration seems far removed from the bewilderment of loss. Do we hope that celebration will spare us? Do we think, in our wildly hopeful hearts, that we can dodge this bullet? We have forgotten what Samuel Johnson knew about human sorrow: that it requires what it cannot hope, that the laws of the universe should be repealed, that the dead should return, that the past should be recalled. We have, I believe, lost a certain *gravitas*—a weight of sorrow. Not that celebration is a bad thing; the Irish, with their singing and wailing, eating and drinking, seem to have it down just right.

In Judaism, life always takes precedence over death. If a funeral procession meets a wedding procession at the cross-roads, the wedding procession always has the right of way. But then again, the rabbis have a few qualifications: this applies only if there are not sufficient people at the funeral procession. And how many are sufficient? *Twelve thousand men and six thousand trumpets,* saith Samuel.

"The disconsolate are the masters of consolation," says American writer and critic Leon Wieseltier. "They offer sympathy without illusion." Sorrow, he says, wants nothing but sorrow.

———

"Think," muses my friend Miriam, "what we lost when we changed our parlours into TV rooms." The parlour, from *parler* "to speak," was a room for private conversations; it was the room we were not allowed to enter—the room with floral settees, heavy drapes and a piano with sheet music propped up on the closed keyboard. A room of awkward suitors and afternoon teas, and the one room in the house where visitors would come to pay their respects to the body laid out in an open casket on a catafalque beside a slightly open window. The large-scale use of funeral homes, or funeral parlours, changed the connotation of the word *parlour* as a room in the house. No longer would a parlour in a person's home be associated with a wake, death or mourning, but it could now be a room for the living, or *living room*. The room that was off limits to us is now the room of the flat screen and the recliner.

We have become uneasy, almost indifferent mourners. No women in black wailing for us. No throwing ourselves on our loved ones' graves or climbing into the coffin, as my friend's daughter did when her father died. No husband like the one in the German film *Cherry Blossoms* who, when his wife dies before her dream of visiting Japan is realized, dresses in her clothing and turns circles beneath the blossoms falling like snow in Tokyo.

If there are two mourners, ruled Hayyim ben Isaac in the late thirteenth century, "the one should leave his house and visit the other." This morning, browsing through the obituaries in the paper, I notice that nearly every one ends with an invitation to email the funeral home with condolences for the family. One of the funeral home sites I check has an online guest book; if you click on a name, you can live-stream the funeral. In the West, we extend our condolences in lieu of consolation. Sympathy in lieu of solace. Sympathy relies on words—Hallmark cards with their sentimental clichés; solace has a more muscular reliance on silence. For those who are connected, hundreds of friends offer condolences on Facebook, and, should you need it, there is an online site with hints on how to express sympathy: *say something simple or admit you don't have a clue what to say and for heaven's sake keep your religious beliefs to yourself.*

I admit to a bias: it is better, I think, that one should leave one's house and visit the other. That we should *go with some show of inconvenience.* That we should *sit openly to weather as to grief.* When I ask my daughter, Leigh, who is well versed in social media, about her thoughts on virtual condolences, she says she understands that her generation turns to Facebook almost reflexively when there is a death. "There is an instant response," she says. "The intention to console is there, but there is no longevity." Online condolences are written for a public audience; once sent, they simply become the latest post. CBC reporter Colleen Ross was shocked to find out that a friend she hadn't seen for several years had died. When she checked on Facebook, she found pages of condolences, some of which were written directly to her friend: "OMG . . . RIP SOOOO sorry to hear of your passing." "Luv n thoughts r w u, I hope u r @ peace wherever u r."

What, I wonder, would the good Hayyim ben Isaac have made of that?

Architects of Loss

When Claudia was a young woman living in Canberra, a friend of hers died suddenly after mistakenly eating an Angel of Death, or death cap mushroom. Nobody in their group of friends had a clue how to organize a funeral, says Claudia, "but the words *duty of care* came to us somehow." Three words that guided everything they did for their friend in the short period of time they had to do it in. I thought about this after she told me, thought about the tension inherent in those three words: a tug between the obligation embedded in *duty* and the implied tenderness lying dormant in *care*. Joined in the middle by a preposition expressing a relationship between a part and a whole. Between what we do and how we do it.

The strangers who will handle our bodies and prepare them for burial or cremation are invisible to us. We don't see them until we need them. Their work is the subject of horror films and ghost stories. We don't dwell too much on the details—what they do or how they do it—we just know that, at some point in our lives, we will call them or someone will call them on our behalf. Over the years I worked with the dying, I became curious about the people who arrived at all hours of the day and night to pick up the bodies of the deceased, and curious about how the dead were treated. In particular, I wondered what happens to the most vulnerable amongst us.

In Amsterdam every year, up to twenty people die anonymously. They come from all walks of life: educated, uneducated, some criminals—drug mules and murderers—

some who just fell on hard times, their bodies found on the streets, in canals, in empty shipping containers and rooming houses. Most are poor, but not all; some have simply outlived everybody in their lives. There is nobody to claim their bodies or bury them—a fact so distressing to civil servant Ger Frits that, twenty-five years ago, he started conducting what have now become known as lonely funerals. At the Saint Barbara Chapel, on a quiet street at the edge of town, Frits has held over five hundred services to say goodbye on behalf of the community when there is nobody else to do so. He places flowers on the casket at the front of the church and chooses one of his favourite classical pieces to play. He hires four pallbearers, and in recent years he has been accompanied by the poet Frank Starik, who was so taken by the idea that he approached Frits in 2002 and has been writing a poem for each funeral ever since. *Goodbye stranger,* he wrote at his first service,

> *I say goodbye on the road to nowhere*
> *To the final country where everyone is welcomed in*
> *Where nothing need know your origin.*

It doesn't matter to Ger Frits that there will be nobody to see the flowers that he brings. "These flowers are not for me, they are not for visitors, they are for the person who passed away," he says with a hint of irritation in his voice. "It's for respect." Neither man is religious, although Frits laughs when he says it can't hurt for someone to put a good word in at heaven's gate.

Farewell sir,
Without papers, without identity.
What were you looking for?
How much did you lose along the way?

Strangers today have come to represent the "other." We see them sleeping in doorways and hear about them stealing our children; in cities, we walk amongst strangers forgetting that, to others, we are the stranger. A couple of times a year I'm called to the ICU to try to help find the family of an unidentified patient. Most often they are males; some have identification, most don't. Sometimes we find a distant relative, someone with whom contact was lost or severed years ago; sometimes there are no leads at all, and the person dies without anybody to notify.

One of our essential qualities, says Starik, is our need for story. He believes the lonely funerals return stories to the people who somehow lost them along the way. What story can I tell about the critically ill, unidentified patients I'm sometimes called to see? The only story left is the story of their death. In the end, we are distilled to the smallest physical detail. Nurses record the minutiae of final hours on the chart: blood pressure, oxygen level, level of consciousness, heart rate, time of death. Sometimes they write that it was quiet and they sat with the patient in the middle of the night. Once, when a woman was taking her last breaths, her estranged son called and we put the phone to her ear and he was able to speak to her on her way out. The last thing she heard was her son's voice. Most often, nobody calls.

In North Vancouver in the 1950s, church bells tolled

regularly for funeral services. It was not unusual for shop owners to close their doors for a couple of hours to attend the funeral of a friend, or for community members to go to the service of someone they'd heard about but had never met. The "strange" who lived amongst us were not necessarily strangers. Every day "Nature Boy," a man in his fifties, shirtless, with a long matted beard, rumoured to live in a cave at the foot of Grouse Mountain, ran barefoot by our house. Eccentricity and danger were not inextricably linked. The woman who lived three doors down from us painted large canvases all night and wore a nun's habit during the day. When she died, the whole neighbourhood came out to say goodbye.

The problem of what to do with the bodies of strangers is at least as old as the Bible. In the past, the poor were often buried in potter's fields — tracts of land that were worthless for growing food. The original one, known as the Field of Blood, is believed to have been in the clay-rich Hinnom Valley in Jerusalem — bought with the thirty pieces of silver that Judas Iscariot was paid to betray Jesus and which he returned to the priests before hanging himself. With that money, the priests *took counsel, and bought with them the potter's field, to bury strangers in* (Matthew 27:7). In Ross Bay Cemetery, the oldest cemetery in Victoria, Section F, known as a potter's field, was used mostly for the destitute, the unidentified, stillborn babies and convicts.

I call Lorraine again, at the Royal Oak Burial Park, to ask what happens to the unidentified and others who die alone in Victoria; what, I wonder, do contemporary potter's fields look like? I now think of Lorraine as my "source." I expect to hear that the bodies are cremated or buried in mass graves, but am surprised when she tells me they are buried throughout the cemetery in the most economical areas, generally along the perimeter on the roadside, but she tries whenever possible to choose a good site. She buries the young close to each other. "I like to nestle them together," she says. There was nothing on these graves when Lorraine started working ten years ago, but each now has a flower vase and most have small concrete markers. Infants are buried in fraction plots all over the park—tucked into the little spaces between graves.

The first funeral Lorraine attended at Royal Oak was for a man who had outlived his family and friends but who had left detailed instructions in his will as to how to conduct his funeral, including which hymns to play and scriptures to read, along with the kind of casket and the flowers he wanted placed on top. Lorraine made sure everything was done as he wanted, and then she dressed in a suit and attended the funeral along with the minister who gave the service. The two of them in the empty church. In the past, whenever she drove the coach for the funeral of a homeless person, she made sure to wear her white gloves as a sign of respect. I am surprised to find out there are lonely funerals being conducted so close to home. *Who, then, loved you? In which rooms did you sleep, who kissed you good night?*

———

"If we find a mound six feet long and three feet wide in the forest, formed into a pyramid, shaped by a shovel, we become solemn and something tells us: somebody lies buried here.— This is architecture!" So said the Austro-Hungarian architect

Adolf Loos. From the small family plots that are disappearing on the prairies to the monuments that hold human history—Yad Vashem in Jerusalem, "the Wall" in Washington, D.C., the Memorial to the Disappeared in Santiago, Chile, through public memorials such as Strawberry Fields in Central Park—architecture is an art form that uses light and space as its raw materials and points to the dwelling places of the living and the dead. As with poetry, it is a kind of translation—of the world and ourselves in it. Not all—but some—architects are poets.

How does one begin to create a space for the dead? What thoughts come? How is it different from creating a space for the living? For some people, a place to remember the dead is important; for others, it is of no consequence. The Bedouin are said to bury their dead in the desert with anonymous and temporary markers that the sands efface over time. Their home, then, becomes the desert itself—the shifting sands forming and reforming in a way that makes spirit visible.

I first met Bill Pechet at the Woods Columbaria in Capilano View Cemetery in West Vancouver, where we went for a walk together. At the entrance to the Columbaria, which he designed, is a concrete seat—"a bus stop for ghosts," laughs Pechet—above which these lines from a poem by the late John Glassco are engraved on a granite slab: *Think of the refuge, the point of sky, the certain castle, the certain presence.* Ringed by salal, huckleberry, ferns, hemlock and fir, the clusters of columbaria—or little niches for cinerary urns—are topped with concrete roofs shaped like old funerary beds, and the clusters, each holding the ashes of fifty-six people, have names such as Cypress, Moss and Salal—"so that people can feel they are resting in a home with a name," says Pechet.

According to Catholic tradition, ashes must be placed in sepulchral vaults with recesses in the walls—from the Latin *columbarius*, "a nesting place for pigeons." The ashes of our loved ones are tucked safely in dovecotes. Cemeteries everywhere are inhabited by small flocks of the dead.

I ask Bill what's involved in creating a home for the dead and he tells me there is a great freedom to be found when the body is not confined by the conventional space of the living world: "We do not need to worry about whether it will be able to walk up a set of stairs or turn on the light in the garage." In the midst of a cemetery laid out with flat stones, he has created a refuge. On a sunny day, when you stand in the middle of the site and look up, the second-growth firs and hemlocks circling the columbaria narrow to a point of blue sky. Throughout the site, small pools catch rainwater so that the sky is reflected at eye level. This is, quite simply, the poetry of death. A few of the niches have mirrors in them so that when you look in, you see your reflection.

My brother lies buried amidst a sea of flat stones. The only thing visible on the manicured lawns are the people standing at the graves. In that graveyard, the mourners stand out like prey. Bill, a soft-spoken, humble man, believes the physical and emotional needs of the mourner or the visitor are most often overlooked; as much as possible he tries to create spaces that honour the corporeal self—that pay attention to sight, touch, sound.

The memorialization of babies poses a particular challenge. Until recently, infants were often buried in separate sections in graveyards, along with convicts and the unidentified. In *Tess of the D'Urbervilles*, Tess gathers some flowers, tips the sexton with a shilling and a pint of beer, and buries her baby by lantern-light in the churchyard in the dead of night "in that shabby corner of God's allotment where he lets the nettles grow and where all unbaptized infants, notorious drunkards and suicides and others of the conjecturally damned are laid." In *The Book of Oaths*, written in 1649, midwives were instructed to bury a baby in such a secret place "as neither Hogg nor Dogg, nor any other beast may come unto it." When babies are born under twenty weeks, the parents can choose to have the hospital "dispose" of the body; over twenty weeks, it is up to the parents to take care of arrangements.

In English folklore, unbaptized babies are said to become butterflies or moths, pixies and will-o'-the-wisps. In one of his most recent projects, the Little Spirits Garden at Royal Oak Burial Park, it would seem that Bill and his partners have tapped into that magic thinking. Little concrete spirit houses in a wooded grove signify individual losses, while clusters of the houses, scattered throughout the site, are visible evidence of a community of mourners. This tiny village will memorialize over three thousand babies. In the trees above the houses are thin wood-veneer sheets on which people can write messages or hang little bells or beads. The *wind notes*, as they are known, move in the breeze the way mobiles move over the heads of babies in their cribs.

It is Remembrance Day today. When I was a girl, my mother and I would dress up and walk to the cenotaph in Victoria

Park, where we'd stand a short distance away from the veterans in their blue blazers and berets and watch as wreaths were laid at the base of the memorial. At the time, I didn't understand that the granite monument was symbolically an *empty tomb* honouring those whose remains were elsewhere. The death of a loved one has more to do with the phantom limb than the amputation. "What replaces the body," says Bill Pechet, "is its absence." What is gone still has form; the space that was once occupied is, not unlike the non-existent limb, a shape forged on the anvil of memory. There is nothing as silent as the room in which the newly dead lie. We hear both the absence of sound—gone the laboured breathing and congestion, the intermittent breaths—and the presence of silence. The absence of sound is what is taken away; the presence of silence is what replaces it. In this silence, we listen with a kind of wonder.

From lonely funerals to strange fairy-tale memorials, there are people who spend their days giving absence a form: caring for the dead, speaking for them when there is nobody left to do so, washing their bodies, dressing them, burying and cremating them, and daydreaming about where they will live and how they will build a home for them. People who work at creating spaces where, if we listen, we might hear the dead speak to us.

I am deeply moved by the individuals who work to honour the dead; and yet, as a society, we often fail miserably. An article in the *Globe and Mail* in early November 2012 revealed that a federal burial fund, called the Last Post Fund, meant to assist impoverished veterans with the cost of a funeral, has rejected more than two-thirds of the applications it's received since 2006. Traditionally, the last post is a bugle call played as a final farewell symbolizing that the dead can rest in peace. According to the executive director of the fund, the government just doesn't see this as a priority. What does this say about us? What, one wonders, have we forgotten?

It matters how we care for the dead; how we navigate between duty and care, obligation and tenderness. We are not separate from the dead—we carry them with us. And they carry us. Surely we are their guardians just as they are ours.

On Remembrance Day 2005, a group of First Nations elders, veterans and youth travelled to Ypres and Normandy to conduct "calling home ceremonies" to invite the spirits of those who had died overseas to return to their homelands and rest with their ancestors in Canada. Calling the dead the way my mother stood on the porch on early summer evenings and called out my name until I reluctantly stopped playing and followed her voice home.

How do we call our own dead? And, when we call them, where do we call them home to?

A. L. KENNEDY'S BOOK ON BULLFIGHTING OPENS WITH HER SIT-ting on her window ledge four storeys above the street contemplating suicide. She is saved from herself by the sound of a man's voice singing "Mairi's Wedding" in the distance, a song she hated with a vengeance as a child. Murdering myself, she thinks, to this accompaniment is more than I can bear. She climbs back inside her apartment and, sorting through her potential projects, decides to take up an assignment writing about bullfighting in Spain.

On the way to her first bullfight, Kennedy catches a southbound sleeper train from Madrid's Atocha station to Granada. The same train that Federico García Lorca took, against all advice, on the night of July 13, 1936, when he left the safety of Madrid for the uncertainty and danger of his home in Granada. The silver-leaved olive groves and terraced rows of almond trees would have been much the same, but the wind turbines are new. Lorca would not have seen those giants turning cartwheels like acrobats on the hills or heard their steady hum like the thrum of ten thousand blackbirds in the air. Less than a month after arriving at the Huerta de San Vicente in Granada, he was executed by a Nationalist death squad and tossed into an unmarked grave.

When Kennedy leaves Granada to return to Madrid, she takes the night train. "Although this is stupid and pointless," she writes, "I want to leave on his behalf . . . I want to reverse that last sleeping-car journey Lorca made to come home — unravelling the mistake, sleeper by sleeper, back to Atocha Station, Madrid."

There is no such unravelling I can do for my brother. Like the twelfth fairy in "The Sleeping Beauty," I want to change the curse of death to a peaceful sleep, but I have no such power. I have imagined sitting with him, holding him, on the wet road outside Toronto before help arrived, but this is a sentimental exercise: we do not meet there. If anything, we meet in this roving collection of my thoughts on death. He appears, unbidden, when I least expect him.

I was getting ready for bed when the ambulance attendants were lifting up his broken body. I hope he felt safe in the arms of the stranger who must have appeared as an angel whether or not one believes in them. I hope that he saw the Pleiades, or Seven Sisters, flung out above him. In ancient times, it was believed that the veil dividing the living from the dead was at its thinnest point when the stars of the Pleiades reached their highest point in the sky. I hope that his father was there waiting as fathers have waited patiently for their sons forever. When Priam comes to Achilles, in book twenty-four of the Iliad, asking for his son's body to be returned to him, Achilles agrees for no reason other than human decency. He replies that all will be done as requested and takes the aged king by the right hand at the wrist, so that his heart might have no fear.

I hope that the last person to touch my brother was tender, and if they arrived when he was taking his last breaths I hope one of them touched his right hand at the wrist, so that his heart might have no fear.

FOUR

Death's Confidante

Events, far-reaching enough to people all space, whose end is nonetheless tolled when one man dies, may cause us wonder.
—JORGE LUIS BORGES, *Dreamtigers*

Last Visit

On a summer day in 2005, I visited my last hospice patient at 3602 Shelbourne Street in one of the complexes for seniors known as retirement communities. There was nothing dramatic about the visit; rather, I remember how ordinary death had become. The nurse and I walked into the lobby and introduced ourselves as the palliative care team—three words that magically cleared the way for us to enter gated and private residences—as if death itself had come to call. We made our way to the elevator, past the lunch menu on a blackboard beside the desk and the fake waterfall with tropical plants in a corner of the room, and rode to the sixth floor, where we got off and walked down a long carpeted hallway to room 601.

There was not a lot for me to do on this visit; the patient lived on her own and had a twenty-four-hour home support worker to help bathe her and give medications. The apartment was full of death's paraphernalia: drinking glasses with labelled syringes, laxatives and anti-emetics, a walker, a raised toilet seat and handrails in the bathroom, an oxygen tank with its serpentine hose coiled in the bedroom, and a tackle box full of medications on the kitchen counter. The patient, in a Red Cross bed, was in a coma and very peaceful. I looked around the living room at the photos of her grandchildren, the crocheted pillows, the glass cabinet with its delicate glass figurines and willow-patterned china, and I felt indifferent. I had overstayed my welcome in death's house. I had more acquaintances amongst the dead than amongst the living. My mother-in-law believed a long parade of ghosts followed me like the tail of a kite wherever I went.

That afternoon, the cheers from a nearby soccer game, the smell of car exhaust, and of pizzas from the joint across the street, the slow wave of a sprinkler arcing across dry grass and the first autumn leaves hanging from the poplars all seemed to be part of the quotidian world—a world where not everybody I met was going to die a few days or weeks after I met them. That's it, I thought, I'm done with death, as I closed the door and walked out into the glare of the afternoon feeling strangely mortal.

In those first days and weeks, sitting in my backyard, it was too soon to think about what I remembered; too soon to wonder about what I'd forgotten. It was enough to sit outside in the sun and begin to find my way back to the uneventful.

For a long time, my involvement with hospice was not just work, it was a calling. Not a religious call, although one can't do the work without a deep sense of the mystery that surrounds the dying. Rather, it was the thing I did that made me feel most alive.

In order to be with the dying, I found it necessary to call upon everything: weeks I had spent at sea on ships with men whose language I did not understand, the arrivals in new ports at dawn and the departures in the dead of night when the heaviness of sleep lay over the harbour like a fog; the grain elevators where my brother shot squab and trains pulled into the yards with their golden cargo. I needed the disorientation of falling in love, the births of my children, the dissolution of my marriage and the rediscovery of poetry, books I had read and forgotten, and a song, one night, rising from a burnt church; I needed the woman who slept on her son's grave and the other woman who never visited the cemetery where her son was buried; the little funerals on my mother's lawn and the funeral my brother never had. I needed to understand what it was to be alive before I could begin to comprehend what it might be like to die.

"For the sake of a single poem," wrote Rilke, "you must see many cities, many people and things, you must understand animals, must feel how birds fly and know the gesture which small flowers make when they open in the morning. You must be able to think back to streets in unknown neighbourhoods, to unexpected encounters, and to partings you had long seen coming."

I needed the war stories, including the one in which my mother was trapped in the rubble of a bombed-out house in London for thirty hours with the body of her mother, and other war stories about dancing all night in a ballroom where blackout curtains darkened the city like a closed eyelid and it was easy to fall in love with the boys who were leaving the next morning. I needed to understand how romance was sharpened by the proximity of death and how it was possible to survive when all one loved was lost.

It was necessary to put away all that I had learned in school, to forget the theories and techniques, the models of grief and the stages of recovery, in order to give them time to turn into glance and gesture; to feel the work in my blood and not in my head. What I learned in school, to put it simply, was necessary but not particularly helpful. In the same way that poetry calls upon all that one knows and all that one has forgotten, so too does being in the presence of death. I knew I was in trouble when, having left one patient, I heard myself thinking, Next.

In 1985, death felt like a new frontier. Palliative care was just starting in Canada, with the first hospices opening in 1975 at St. Boniface Hospital in Winnipeg and at the Royal Victoria Hospital in Montreal. Victoria Hospice opened in 1980, and in those first years it felt as if we were renegades on the outskirts of the medical establishment. We had to learn the language of the dying and understand that the place they inhabited was a new world, a place we could never fully enter. "We had to be explorers," says counsellor Elizabeth Causton, "willing to go into uncharted areas, to be surprised by what was around the next bend." We brought our humanity and our eccentricities to the work. And sometimes we brought our own brand of black humour. Called to the home of Harry Tether, a ninety-year-old man who was very close to death, my friend Heather Fox thought, when she saw him lying still in his bed, that he had died before the team arrived. She sat with him for a while and then quietly said, "You know, if I had married you, my name would be Heather Tether." Within a minute or so his shoulders began to shake and he started to laugh and ended up not dying that day after all.

We never knew what a visit would bring or what would

be needed. We just went, as the saying goes, with the flow. On a visit to a First Nations man with leukemia who had been in pain for hours, the team arrived and before they could do anything, he asked his wife, "Have you shown them the smokehouse?" His wife, startled, said no, but agreed to take the two women outside to see the fish smoking in the shed. When they returned to the living room, he looked at them and then at his wife and said, "You didn't leave them in long enough, they're still white!" They all laughed and for the briefest moment he was a man with a sense of humour and not just a man dying of a devastating illness.

For a long time the intensity and immediacy of my encounters with the dying and their families made working with death a kind of seduction. Small talk fell away, each visit was intimate; the work was unpredictable, mysterious, difficult and wondrous. When people found out what I did for a living, the response was inevitably something along the lines of, "I could never do that!" and even though I would never admit to it, to be seen doing something others couldn't even imagine doing pleased me. I felt as if I belonged to a secret society. The work felt important. I was not an angel—none of us were—but damn, it was hard to imagine what else I might do. The heartbreak and grace, despair and fear, the moments of synchronicity and wonder placed all of us—the dying and the living—at the heart of the human story. What could be more seductive than that? And yet I felt increasingly as if I was walking with ghosts, wandering the dark corridors— pinned somewhere between commitment and wariness, between feeling fully alive and profoundly exhausted.

Caught between the mechanics of dying and the mystery

of death, what stories can I tell you about my travels through these lands? To be employed to help people die is a kind of aberration, a deviation from the way things used to be done, when the dying were cared for at home by family members and the body was laid out and washed by the local women; when the trajectory from being alive to being dead was a more visible one and a death set in motion a chain reaction in the kitchens of mourners, who arrived with piping hot dishes on the doorstep and matter-of-fact offers of help to mow the lawn or walk the dog or take the kids to their swimming lessons. This is not to take away from the skill and compassion of the people who care for the dying and the dead, but to wonder what it means for us all when the last hands to touch us will most likely be those of a stranger. And to wonder, as well, what it means when the sheer volume of death encountered by those who do the work makes the job comparable to working in a war zone.

The language of vicarious traumatization is useless. *The Handbook on Self-Care* says three things will help: escape, rest and play. Not a lot of room in that, says my friend Miriam, "for subtle agony or unwished-for blessings, for sanctity and profanity. Not a lot of room to describe the kind of sex we have after bathing the dead or being present to the revulsion of vomit, blood, rot." Every death I saw was a kind of dress rehearsal. When somebody my age was dying, I looked for those same symptoms in myself. I developed a kind of catastrophic thinking: the smallest symptom was easily interpreted as a death sentence. I would go through periods of visiting my doctor more regularly, only to have him smile and ask, "What body part are we cutting off today?"

Twenty-two years ago, when I moved into the house I'm living in now, one of the first things I did was look around to see where a Red Cross bed would best fit on the main floor. It didn't occur to me until years later that this might not be on the typical homeowner's list of things to think about.

I find myself struggling to come up with answers, as if, having gone to the land of death and dying, I should have returned with something to say, some nugget of wisdom to ease fear or make the transition easier. Am I more or less afraid of death, having hung out with it backstage for years, you might wonder? Did the rehearsals ease the terror of what it will be like—to use a corny metaphor—to step out on opening night? Everybody has a death story. We are equally fascinated and horrified by the details; we tell our stories as if they can walk us through fear towards some kind of understanding.

I am no longer as innocent as I was. If anything, my fear has more shape now. I have more ways to describe and name the ways in which I could die. And yet, more than dying, I fear leaving: this earth, the people I love, the joys and struggles of my children that I will not be a part of. I fear being the cause of grief that at the same time I am unable to console. I fear a disease that will make me a stranger long before death finally arrives—like the man I met with a brain tumour who, having been gentle his whole life, became violent with his wife and unrecognizable to himself. As most people do, I fear becoming a burden or losing my mind, like another man I met with early-onset dementia who believed himself to be a fish. (On second thought, as tragic as that was, it would most likely amuse my children no end.) I fear the shock of an initial diagnosis and all the uncertainty of what to do or not do; I fear that hope might blind me, like the thief it is, to whatever time remains. I think of my friend looking around her apartment and asking, "How do I leave this?" After years of being with the dying, I still have no answer for her.

When I was just starting out, I watched a woman with a death's head insignia on the back of her fringed jacket cradle a dying boy in her lap and I wanted to be as fearless as she was. I wanted to walk into death's house and put my feet up on death's coffee table. In the end, even though I learned to walk towards death, I was never fearless. My anxieties had to do with the sounds and smells of dying, with the gasping breaths or the possibility of a sudden bleed—anxieties that belong to the living and not necessarily, as I came to see over time, to the dying.

"It is impossible to imagine our own death," wrote Freud, "and whenever we attempt to do so, we can perceive that we are in fact still present as spectators." What we see and feel at the bedside, as observers—the immensity of loss, the shutting down of the body, our own grief and helplessness—is not always the same for the dying, who in some miraculous way often appear to be spared the full knowledge of the reality of their death. I don't know how this works, but over and over again I saw the dying in what appeared to be an altered state. Whereas the living see the past, the present and the future—see what is being lost, how it is being lost and what will no longer be—the perspective of the dying appears less expansive, as if, preparing to enter a narrow space, their focus becomes more immediate. It is a state not unlike that of marathon runners for whom endorphins kick in as they near the end of a race, leaving some calm, some elated, some euphoric.

In his last hours, D. H. Lawrence, feeling as if he was floating away, is said to have cried out for Aldous Huxley to hold his ankles. On his deathbed, Aldous Huxley, no longer able to speak, scribbled a note to his wife asking for an intramuscular injection of LSD—while in the next room, unbeknownst to him, coverage of President John F. Kennedy's assassination was being broadcast on the TV. While he was dying, Huxley's wife whispered, "willingly and consciously you are going, willingly and consciously, and you are doing this beautifully—you are going toward the light—you are going toward a greater love. You are going toward Maria's [Huxley's first wife, who had died many years earlier] love with my love. You are going toward a greater love than you have ever known. You are going toward the best, the greatest love, and it is easy, it is so easy, and you are doing it so beautifully." One hopes that Huxley's last high was a mind-bending, psychedelic passage through the gates of perception. It would have been a real bummer, as the saying went in the sixties, if he ended up having a bad trip with his last hit of acid.

There are two realities in the rooms of the dying—that of the people gathered around the bedside and that of the person close to death—and they are often as different from each other as night from day. In his Mennonite community on the prairies, Patrick's uncle Henry was a sitter for the dying. When there was no immediate family available, Henry would sit at the bedside so that the person would not be alone. When he was imminently dying, Henry sat up and became suddenly sociable, as if welcoming the ones who had gathered into his living room. When it was his turn, Henry became a sitter for the living—putting them at ease on his deathbed.

I don't know if the drugs used to combat pain or shortness of breath or restlessness are fully responsible for the altered state of the dying. I don't know if there is some chemical that gets released near the end of the race that allows us to be less afraid than we think we might be. YES, reads the headline in the *New York Times*, RUNNING CAN MAKE YOU HIGH. If we think of ourselves as marathon runners getting high on endorphins the closer we get to the finish line, well, that takes a bit of the sting out of the whole end-of-life conundrum.

In her judgment striking down the ban against assisted suicide in the spring of 2012, Justice Lynn Smith, of the B.C. Supreme Court, wrote, "Palliative care, though far from universally available in Canada, continues in its ability to relieve suffering. However, even the very best palliative care cannot alleviate all suffering, except possibly through sedation to the point of persistent unconsciousness." The question of alleviating suffering is an old one. Ten thousand years ago, the practice of trepanation—drilling a hole in the skull with a flint knife to release trapped spirits—was practised in Turkey. In the sixties, John Lennon proposed to Paul McCartney that they have the procedure done. To which the saner Beatle replied, "Look, you go and have it done, and if it works, great. Tell us about it and we'll all have it." We have tried to relieve suffering by seeking certainty, moving from polytheism to monotheism in our search for the one God who might help us—if not in this world then in the next. Religion tells us there is a purpose to suffering—a purpose that we might not understand but one that is known to a higher power. Whole treatises have been written on suffering by people whose knowledge of it is intimate. Paul Celan, Viktor Frankl, Elie Wiesel, Tzvetan Todorov and Primo Levi, amongst others, have all given voice to the atrocities experienced in Second World War concentration camps, and yet suffering, by its very nature, is an experience that is deeply private and nearly impossible to fully communicate to others. In a contemporary world where *no pain, no gain*, is a modern mini-narrative, suffering has come to be linked to a kind of exhibitionism and is often portrayed in our cultural psyche as something that needs to be "fixed." I am not sure it is possible to completely alleviate suffering; I doubt that it is.

In the late 1990s, I met a woman who had come to Canada from Holland to care for her sister, who was struggling through the last weeks of her dying. She told me how, in Holland, when her husband was diagnosed with cancer, she went with him to the doctor to request help in ending his life. The doctor told them it was too early, that they would regret making the decision while there was still quality time left. They went away and lived as fully as they could until her husband was very close to death, and then the woman returned to the doctor and was given three pentobarbital suppositories. She gave the first one to her husband and he died peacefully before the others could be administered. The time between when he would have died of natural causes and his "assisted" death was short enough to be barely discernible; what mattered was the knowledge they both had that they had some control over his last days. This woman did not understand why her sister, who had been in a coma for over a week, and who depended on home support workers to bathe her and empty her catheter and turn her to avoid bedsores, was not allowed to die peacefully a little ahead of schedule.

The focus on relieving suffering and providing a good quality of life as one approaches death is of enormous benefit; and yet, in the end, I left the work thinking that although palliative care is an invaluable piece of what is needed, it is not the only answer, and in Canada, where only 16 to 30 percent of dying patients receive palliative care, it is not even an option for many people. My experience was with people dying of terminal illnesses. The metaphoric language, altered states, the turning away from this life and the spiritual encounters that often happened close to death are all related to palliative deaths. There is no promise of a good death—with or without somebody to help us in our last days; there is only our perception of what our death might be. In the end, there are no definitive answers. No all-encompassing truths about death and how we die. Exposure to suffering changes us. Whereas I once thought death had its own timetable, I now think there can be great peace of mind when we have some say in the timing of our own death. "I'm deeply grateful," Gloria Taylor, one of the plaintiffs in the B.C. Supreme Court ruling, told reporters, "to have the comfort of knowing that I'll have a choice at the end of my life." The words *comfort* and *choice* seem like good words to have in mind when considering one's own death.

To work with the dying was to enter the darkness without a map of the way home; to merge, briefly, with something greater than myself. It was to understand that while suffering could not be eliminated, it was possible, for brief periods, to try to inhabit it; to be present, often without a clue what to do—to accompany the dying as far as possible and to stand alone under the stars they disappeared into.

Robert Pogue Harrison, professor of literature at Stanford and author of *The Dominion of the Dead*, writes: "As *Homo sapiens* we are born of our biological parents. As human beings we are born of the dead—of the regional ground they occupy, of the languages they inhabited, of the worlds they brought into being." We are not separate from the dead; we carry them with us. And they carry us. My brother, the woman whose bones broke like twigs, the boy dying of AIDS. My mother. The innumerable others.

"We had to be explorers," said Elizabeth. And, we were.

The Mountaintop

A few years ago, I was invited to take part in a discussion about the artist and mortality at the University of British Columbia's Green College. The evening, organized by writer-in-residence Don Hannah, centred on the question *Why do we make art about death?* Of all the reasons I thought of— for love, for beauty, to bridge our aloneness, to face our fears, to leave evidence of our existence in red ochre on cave walls, to defy death, to transform it, translate it, transcend it—the one that resonated most deeply with me was the idea that art frees us from the literal. Art is the imagination's take on death. It looks beyond the physical decline of our bodies to the mystery of our leaving. It allows angels to crash through the mortar of our ceilings and shows us the face of the Grim Reaper; it makes the invisible visible and invites us into other realities. "Art," wrote the Japanese dramatist Chikamatsu Monzaemon, "is something that lies in the slender margin between the real and the unreal." The same slender margin it could be said that the dying inhabit.

From our very beginnings we have told ourselves stories about death to explain the known, the unknown and the unknowable. Last year, in New York, my daughter and I went to see *The Mountaintop*, a two-person play that reimagines Martin Luther King Jr.'s last night on earth. In room 306 at the Lorraine Motel in Memphis, Tennessee, on April 3, 1968, Dr. King returns to his room on a stormy night, having just delivered the brilliant "I've Been to the Mountaintop" speech at the Mason Temple in support of a sanitation workers' strike. The second character, a cigarette-smoking, hard-drinking maid, turns out, as the play progresses, to be a rookie angel on her first assignment: to tell the preacher he will be shot the next day and to prepare him for the journey into what Hamlet calls *the undiscovered country*.

We meet in the slender margin between myth and reality, fiction and non-fiction. When some critics wrote that the play was not believable, I was flabbergasted. Why not a boozy, foul-mouthed angel to see us out? Why not an angel with strands of humanity still hanging on, an angel who knows the life of matter, of earthly existence?

Art, says Tennessee Williams, is the one way we have to arrest time. Death masks in the eighteenth and nineteenth centuries preserved the faces of princes, poets, musicians, lunatics and murderers long after death. The Victorians posed with their dead, dressing them up in their best clothes and arranging them in lifelike poses. In the twenty-first century, the sheer volume of our exposure to death in films, news and television programming has trivialized death and resulted in a kind of voyeurism that leaves us strangely removed from death as a reality.

Who will interpret death for us? The artist, the visionary, the psychotic? The dying themselves, around whom mystery is made manifest? To be with the dying is to leave the known world and enter a world of spirit and hallucination, vision and visitation. It is to understand they navigate by dead reckoning: memorizing where they have come from and holding an image of where they are going in their minds while you, standing on the shoreline, watch as they slip the bowline and—guided by the moon, stars, wind, waves, clouds and currents—disappear from this world. It is not to sentimentalize but to remain open to possibility. Perhaps we must all strive to be—as Marianne Moore instructs the poets—*literalists of the imagination*, capable of presenting, when called upon, *imaginary gardens with real toads in them*.

A friend told me about a dream he had a few hours before his wife went into labour with their first baby. Standing on a riverbank beside his late sister, he watched her cast a line in long, slow arcs over the water. When she landed a salmon, she passed the rod to him to reel it in. The fish was magnificent, burnished gold and silver with scales like jewels—like the biggest catfish in the world that Ed Bloom catches the day his son, Will, is born in *Big Fish*. The same fish he turns into at the end of the film when Will carries him to the water and off Edward swims, now the big fish in the large lake of eternity. Like the fish my mother turned into when we scattered her ashes in Burrard Inlet and she disappeared in a flash of what looked like emerald scales beneath the water's slate-grey surface. "A man," says Will, "becomes his stories. They live on after him. And, in that way, he becomes immortal."

We tell ourselves stories, not to romanticize or sentimentalize death, but to guide us and make meaning where we can. My master's thesis was on Coast Salish perceptions of death and dying. In one of my conversations with the elder in the study, we talked about the dead and how they continue to be a part of our lives. "Some dreams," she told me, "are simply dreams; others are visits." For my friend, there was no doubt that his sister had briefly stood with him on the riverbank before all hell broke loose and his baby began to swim like a great fish towards him.

The late Irish writer John Moriarty believed that light blinds us to other realities. Standing in his kitchen with the lights out, he could see the natural light on the water and the rocks and mountains in their dark homes; turn on the light in the kitchen and the world outside disappears. In a radio broadcast he made when he was dying, Moriarty tells of a man who loses the key to his house in the shadows near his door and goes to look for it under a street lamp down the road. A policeman joins him in the search under the circle of light until finally, when he says it's not there and asks where the man lost it, the man replies that the key is in the darkness outside his home. The policeman asks why they are searching where they are and the man says it is the only light around and therefore he will search there.

The key is in the darkness. We must enter it in order to find our way home. We must, as Keats believed, be capable of being in uncertainties, mysteries, doubts, without any irritable reaching after fact or reason. The imagination is infinite; reason is limited. In Barcelona, a city marked by the genius and madness of Antonio Gaudí, the imagination is made visible. Patrick and I walked with our friends Patricia and Terence past balconies with shark eyes, pineapples on church spires, castles and turrets on top of buildings, and when we looked down at the sidewalk, we saw we were walking on starfish. *To go in the dark with a light*, wrote the American poet Wendell Berry, *is to know the light. To know the dark, go dark. Go without sight.*

The slender margin between the real and the unreal is the margin between factual truth and narrative truth. To read the Bible literally is to miss the poetry at the heart of it: *Let the floods clap their hands; let the hills be joyful together* (Psalm 98:8). To approach death literally is also to limit ourselves. The body shutting down is, in and of itself, not mysterious: people sleep more, stop swallowing, have long pauses in breathing; the extremities cool and many people become incontinent, disoriented, congested; and most fall into an abnormal pattern of breathing called Cheyne-Stokes—a type of cyclic breathing that involves fast breaths followed by slower ones punctuated by periods of apnea. The final breath is a shallow exhalation. The factual truth is objective. The narrative truth opens the door to the mysterious.

It is the story we tell ourselves:

> *I was a girl when my brother was killed. In the silence that followed his death, grief took up residence in our house. His death led me to the dying, and death led me back to him.*

Art lies somewhere between the corporeal and the spiritual: the sacred and the profane. I am closest to my mother and brother and innumerable others when I write about them. My friend Jan is a weaver. When she applied for a grant to teach women on her reserve to weave, the band council wanted her to teach women with alcoholism, as this would be good therapy for them. Jan refused. To her, the object of art is not therapy; rather, it is a way of seeing the world, an exploration. In terms of her weaving, it is a way to shake hands with the ancestors and to see the beauty of the world through their eyes.

I did not start this book thinking it would be therapeutic or that it would lead me to my brother; I wrote, as Joan Didion says, to find out what I was thinking. Along the way, I was surprised.

I ARRIVED AN HOUR EARLY AT GREEN COLLEGE. IT WAS A COOL November evening, the ground was littered with red maple leaves; a few students were crossing the campus on their way to night classes. With time to kill, I thought I'd take a stroll. Not knowing the UBC campus, I decided to walk in a straight line, down the East Mall, so that I wouldn't get lost.

How do we find the things we've lost? Do we find them by design or by chance? Do we find them or do they find us?

After walking for twenty minutes, I stopped in front of a well-lit building, and when I asked a student passing by if there was a library nearby, she said, "You're standing beside one." I went in, walked up to the second floor and waited while the librarian helped a young woman. Who knows about timing and chance? Who knows about the Three Princes of Serendip who, upon returning home after a number of years of travelling, created a word to tell their father and his court of all the wondrous things they had seen and experienced, and who knows why I would find myself serendipitously on the campus where my brother studied some fifty years earlier, at a symposium on mortality?

"Can I help you?" the librarian asked.

"I'm not sure," I said. I told her my brother had been a student at UBC in the early sixties and I thought he'd written a thesis but I wasn't sure. That's all I had.

The past seeps into the present like groundwater seeps into the empty spaces and layers of rock upon which we build our worlds. There is no final resolution to loss, but once in a little while some unexpected resonance prompts memories to rustle to the surface, then settle back in a slightly different arrangement—a better arrangement, if that's possible. "Closure," says a friend of mine, "is a crock." We go on with the dead inside us. And sometimes, although it is impossible to explain, it seems they reach out to us.

The librarian found Ian's master's thesis, "The Renaissance Sonneteers," that same night. It was the work of a scholar. I didn't know he'd studied poetry and fallen in love with Wyatt and Surrey, Spenser, Sidney, Shakespeare, Donne and Milton when he was twenty and I was four. I didn't know much; I knew his ghost more than I knew him. I knew the stories I'd been told: how he held court drunk, beautiful, unfit; how he flew planes hundreds of miles off course; how he burned like a brief, brilliant light and was buried in a sky-blue casket on a rainy day when the world as we knew it ended. And the work of mourning—which is the work of remembrance and myth, presence and absence, longing and unanswered questions, ser-endipity and coincidence—began.

When I saw his signature on the front page, I remem-bered copying those elegant loops and scrawls in a lined note-book for pages on end when I was a child. Writing my way towards him then and continuing, as it turns out, through the years to the present day.

Grief, says the Irish writer Colm Tóibín, was not a word that was used in Enniscorthy, County Wexford, when he was grow-ing up—there was only the unspoken experience of it. Poetry, he said, was the language that allowed grief to be expressed. I wrote my first poem shortly after Ian died and gave it to my mother. Where I had no language, poetry spoke for me.

It was clear, reading Ian's thesis, that he had a way of relating to those dead poets, as if he knew them well; sound-ing at times as if he was in a bar with friends. He was just *hanging out with a different crowd. I can see him with John Donne, walking the streets, debating about God and life, writing about him as if he were right there speaking, and then stopping and quoting the poet's pressing question:* What if this present were the world's last night?

AFTERWORD

1964

Joan Didion once famously said, "We tell ourselves stories in order to live." She might just as easily have said, "We tell ourselves stories in order to die." I grew up thinking Ian died when I was twelve—not quite an adolescent but not a child either. I believed he died when the world was coming alive. Nineteen sixty-five. The old order was breaking down. A hundred and twenty-five miles above the earth, Aleksei Leonov opened the door of his spacecraft and stepped out; on the ground, twenty-five thousand civil rights activists marched from Selma, Alabama, to Montgomery; the Beatles played Shea Stadium in New York City and Dylan went electric at the Newport Folk Festival. The old order was breaking down and Ian would have loved that.

It was only in the writing of this book that I discovered he actually died in 1964, when I was eleven. This book started with a lie. We make of death our own mythologies. Did I give myself one extra year with him? Did I give him an extra year so that he too could be in that New World?

"You were twelve," my mother told me.

We all needed to be a little older.

We all needed a little more time.

The Egyptian god of writing, Thoth, has the head of an ibis and carries a writing tablet.

The god of writing I pray to, just in case, is roaring in the heavens, bent over, holding his belly. "You can't *what*?!" he asks incredulously.

I explain to him, patiently, as if I'm explaining something to a drunk, that I don't know how to end this.

"Let me get this right," he says. "You've written a book on death for which there is no ending?"

"That's about it," I mumble. "You do it."

"You're on your own with death," sighs the god. "It's as big a mystery to me as it is to you."

ACKNOWLEDGEMENTS

Heather Fox, Elizabeth Causton, Marg Cooke, Mags Johnston, Susan Auld, Lorna Ross, Lorraine Fracy, Bill Pechet, Claudia Haagen, Don Hannah, Kristin Watson, Eleanor Vincent, Chris Welsh, Joan Tuttle, Beth Shore, Mike Collins, Ivan Pigott, Mike Matthews, Carol Reid, Jamie Reid, Marilyn Lerner, George Bowering.

A special thanks to Michelle Dale for her exquisite thoughts on death and to Alayna Munce for her brilliance.

Patricia and Terence Young for the use of their cabin in the woods and Andreas Schroeder and Sharon Odie Brown for their cottage in Robert's Creek.

Leigh, Lee, Saul, Pauline, Sails, Spencer, Niko, Elisa, Marijke, Pedro and Jonah. Welcome Ava Rose.

First readers: Thea Gray, Scooter Bill, Carol Matthews, Jennifer Fraser, Patricia Young, Lucy Bashford, Dede Crane, Janice McCachen.

To the doctors, nurses, counsellors, volunteers who continue in the work. And to the dying with whom I worked and the dead who are never far away.

Thanks to the B.C. Arts Council and Canada Council.

Thanks to Noelle Zitzer and the staff at HarperCollins, and a special thanks to my superb editor and friend, Patrick Crean.

To my agent extraordinaire, John Pearce, thank you.

And to my partner, Patrick Friesen, for our conversations about death (and everything else) out of which the form of this book emerged. What we started talking about in a doorway those many years ago, and what continues, has deepened my life beyond anything I could have imagined.

In a discussion with the late poet P. K. Page, shortly before her death, we talked about how metaphor, the engine of poetry, is also the language of the dying. She was intrigued and asked if I had written about that. I hadn't. This book is my response to P. K.

SOURCES